Praise for

Most of us see forgiveness as something we ask for and something we give. It takes on the appearance of a commodity in our social transactions. As a result, the inherent value of forgiveness can be lost. In his book, *Forgive.* Jeff Ellis pushes past all of that and opens our minds to a bolder truth. Forgiveness is a law. And a law brings with it certain realities.

God's forgiveness of us is a wonderful and mysterious thing. We can't explain why an all-powerful Creator would be so willing to recognize our faults, our brokenness, our very humanity, and then tell us that He cares about us more than He does any of those things. The beauty and power of *Forgive.* is the revelation that God's invitation for us to be a forgiving people unlocks a timeless law with all of its benefits.

This book was written for me . . . and for you . . . and for every person who has ever walked this earth. By embracing the power God gives us to forgive, we embrace the essence of One who loves more than any other. Forgiving is an act of humility, a removal of self from the center of the universe. When we willfully move from that center, God begins moving our worlds. Forgiveness opens that cosmic portal.

Jeff Ellis, as long as I've known him, has been seeking deeper truth. *Forgive.* allows us to join him on that quest and to discover, first-hand, the homeland that brings us ultimate healing.

Joe L. "Joey" Cope, J.D.
Dean, College of Graduate and Professional Studies
Abilene Christian University

Forgive.

The effects of forgiveness
on *mind, body,* and *spirit.*

Jeffrey Ellis

ISBN-13 9781723308550

For bulk purchase and for booking, contact:

Jeffrey Ellis

jeffellis57@msn.com

Because of the dynamic nature of the Internet, web addresses or links contained in this book may have been changed since publication and may no longer be valid.

Unless otherwise annotated, all scriptures are from the New King James Version of the Bible.

Acknowledgements

The primary editor and inspiration is my wife and partner, Ginger Ellis. She is my continual source of honest feedback, insight, and love.

I would like to acknowledge the special inspiration of Dr. Joey Cope, Lori Anne Shaw, and the Graduate Studies faculty of Abilene Christian University. They encouraged me greatly on this journey and showed me the path of reconciliation and peace.

Finally, my friend and kindred spirit, Everett O'Keefe, has been a tremendous help on this project. I appreciate him and his insights more than I can say.

Dedication

Forgive. is dedicated to our family. As the years have passed by, I find myself atop our family organizational structure, clearly a function of age. Ginger and I have six adult children, some with spouses, who are the loves of our lives. They inspire, surprise, and reward us at every turn. This work is dedicated to this family: Jennifer and Martin Bowers, Justin Ellis and Rachele Brown, Kate and David Schmidgall, Annie and Josh McElroy, Jessie and Abhishek Subhan, and David Ellis.

Also, I would like to dedicate this work to my friend Billy Napp. I hope that you enjoy the scientific adventure that *Forgive.* became for me, and I invite you on the journey. I pray that our Father's love, imagination, and creativity are revealed within these pages.

Introduction

It was a rainy Friday night when Salahuddin called his brother to tell him he was going to make "one last run." Somebody had called for a pizza delivery at the Templeton apartment complex, and Salahuddin was on his way. He arrived at the complex and knocked on the door. The door suddenly flew open, and Trey Relford attacked him with a knife, stabbed him several times, robbed him, and left him to die on the floor. The tender-hearted, hard-working young man had been murdered for pizza money.

Relford was tried and found guilty of killing Salahuddin. At the sentencing hearing, Salahuddin's father had his opportunity to confront the killer. He addressed Relford saying, "Even though you took from me my son, I do not blame you. I am not angry with you at all. *I forgive you for what you have done to Salahuddin and my family.*"

The judge, visibly moved, called for a recess as the attorneys and families tried to compose themselves. The father and Relford unexpectedly met in the middle of the courtroom and embraced, weeping in each other's arms.

Forgiveness is for everyone.

We all need it. And we all need to extend it to others for our own sakes. The good news is that when we forgive others, it heals us. Forgiveness is a universal principle, like gravity. It works for everyone. Because it is God-given, it is God-powered. Like the laws of gravity or thermodynamics, the law of forgiveness is always available and in operation: to help and heal an imperfect people in an imperfect world.

Forgiveness brings us closer to our Maker. No one is too far away to be reached by the love of God. We are not forgotten, and we are not alone. The creator of the universe has set a law in motion that unfailingly draws us to Him and to each other.

Forgiveness draws us closer to one another. Setting aside rights and wrongs, forgiving our friends, families, and strangers, we strengthen our families and communities and reinforce the tie that binds.

We all need it. We all need to give it.

Table of Contents

CHAPTER 1

Forgive

Forgiveness is for everyone.

GOD IS *FOR* US.

He always wants the best for us.

Everyone has been hurt, offended, or abused at one time or another. Perhaps it happened a long time ago, or perhaps the wound is still fresh. In any case, our attitude toward that offending person is having a profound effect on us. Not them, us. When we are bruised and hurt by the conflict of our relationships and the violence of our lives, how do we respond? What can we do to heal our afflictions?

Forgive everyone in our lives.

When we forgive others, we break the bond of bitterness—a powerful bond meant to hold us in the shallows and the shadows. Released from bitterness and blame, we are able to wholly receive what the Lord intends for us: fullness of joy, abundance of Spirit, peace, and grace. When we do forgive someone, it's usually not them who is changed. They may not even be aware of being forgiven. And it doesn't change the offense—what happened, happened. So who does it change? It changes *us*.

The Lord has given us a way to heal ourselves. He created each of us whole and perfect. But our inherited sin causes us to be broken, incomplete, blemished. As Dr. Thomas Bradford writes, "The purpose and goal of redemption is the restoration of wholeness to humanity." God's forgiveness washes us clean and restores us to wholeness. It is how we get back home.

Our lives reflect the choices we've made. Those choices have affected our minds, bodies, and spirits. Forgiveness starts with a decision at which it can be hard to arrive. That decision is often wrapped up in emotion, regret, hurt, and judgment. But once we decide to forgive, it is profoundly simple. We just do it. We deliberately decide in our hearts and minds to release that person from the debt they owe us, from the hurt they caused. Forgiveness is instant.

Forgiveness is an act of grace, not a process. It is immediate and powerful and effective on every level. It doesn't take a committee or prayer chain or multi-step program. It is a decision that each of us makes of our own will. In the simplest terms, forgiveness is the release of a claim against someone else. It's a transaction, sure, but its power reaches the uttermost depths, releasing our hearts from bitterness, anger, and malice. Forgiveness does not come naturally to most of us; rather, anger, bitterness, and resentment come naturally. Forgiveness, if it comes at all, comes supernaturally. And because it is God-breathed, it is God-powered.

God has created a set of laws that govern the universe. These laws affect all of us, whether we believe in God or not. Some govern the physical universe, like the law of gravity, while others are spiritual laws. The law of gravity affects everyone, which is why we don't randomly spin off into space. The gravitational force of 14.7 pounds per square inch applies to everyone and is sufficient to keep us tethered to earth. One of God's spiritual laws is the law of sowing and reaping, which says that "A man reaps what he sows." That law means two things: If we plant corn, we will harvest corn. Second, if we plant sparingly, we will harvest sparingly. And the reverse is also true: If we sow generously, we reap generously. These laws affect everyone, whether we believe in God or not.

The law of forgiveness concerns relationships between people. In October 2017, God told me, "Forgiveness is for everyone." Such a simple statement, but so profound. God has made forgiveness available to the whole world. Like other universal laws, forgiveness works for everyone: believer or non-believer, regardless of race, creed, or color. There is no limit to its healing power.

When the victim forgives the offender, it is a one-sided transaction called unilateral forgiveness. This is not reconciliation. In fact, the offender may not even know they have been forgiven. That's okay. Healing for the victim still happens. Bilateral forgiveness or reconciliation occurs when both parties forgive each other. For our purposes, we will be focusing on unilateral forgiveness.

Here's how it works: when we forgive others, it changes *us*; it changes our hearts. And in that moment, we are healed physically, emotionally, and spiritually. Like so many spiritual truths, forgiveness is a paradox; when we release others, we free ourselves.

CHAPTER 2

Forgiveness & Healing

WHEN WE FORGIVE, the healing effects begin immediately. We feel relieved, like the weight of the world has lifted off our shoulders. Our brains begin flooding our bodies with hormones that counteract the poison of bitterness we have built up inside. Our spirits are lighter, freer, and restored anew.

Throughout the scriptures, forgiveness and healing are linked together. King David wrote, "Look upon my affliction and my pain and forgive all my sins." In Psalm 103, the psalmist writes, "[God] forgives all your iniquities, heals all your diseases." Jesus healed the paralytic, saying, "Son, your sins are forgiven you." Jesus forgave people, and their afflictions vanished. Pastor Bill Johnson of Bethel Church says, "Sickness is to our bodies what sin is to our soul. The atoning work of Jesus dealt with both."

Science is finally demonstrating what we have known by faith: There is deep healing in forgiveness. Researchers tell us that the moment we forgive one another, our bodies begin to release serotonin, dopamine, and oxytocin into our bloodstream. These hormones make us feel relaxed, relieved, and at peace. Serotonin goes to work immediately by relaxing our muscles and improving our blood flow. Our stress levels decrease, and suddenly, our lungs are able to breathe deeply. As those stress levels decrease, our blood pressures and heart rates decrease, and our minds begin to relax. Dopamine floods our brains with feelings of euphoria and well-being.

In the longer run, forgiveness makes us healthier and less prone to disease. Dr. Loren Toussaint of Luther College has found that those who forgive others tend to have "stronger immune systems, less physiological reactivity to stress, lower blood pressure, and overall fewer physical symptoms." Other research suggests that forgiveness may directly improve health by reducing hostility and cardiovascular strain, buffering the immune system through the release of antibodies, and improving the central nervous system functioning.

Cardiovascular health also seems to be improved by forgiveness of others. At the University of Wisconsin, thirty-six Vietnam vets with heart disease were studied. Half the veterans received counselling in forgiveness, and the other half did not. Those who forgave their trespassers showed a "significant increase in the blood flow to their heart muscles." The same study showed that forgiveness also helped prevent heart disease in middle-aged participants. According to the author, in the same study, when the vets showed a high level of forgiveness, they reported fewer heart-related health problems. Conversely, when they showed less forgiveness, they reported a higher incidence of heart disease.

Forgiveness also improves our mental health in powerful ways. Psychologists have only recently recognized the importance of forgiveness. Recent studies indicate that forgiveness can "enhance mental health and reduce depression" and have a protective effect on mental health. That's right. Making forgiveness part of our lives is protective for our minds and bodies against disorders and disease. Researchers are also finding connections between forgiveness and "higher self esteem, lower anxiety, and lower depression." People who are taught to forgive become less angry, more hopeful, less depressed, less anxious, less stressed, more confident, and learn to like themselves more. Almost uniformly, the forgiveness studies show positive results in psychological and emotional well-being.

Physically, emotionally, and mentally, forgiveness is a protective and healing power. Science testifies again and again of the truth of God's word. Being forgiven by God makes us whole. And forgiving others keeps us whole. It is the way we should live.

Brian's Story – as told by his mother, Betty:

May 11, 2004, our son, Brian, was driving home from his college team baseball practice. As a left-handed freshman pitcher with a mean curveball, his future in this sport looked bright. But a minivan suddenly swerved into the intersection and hit Brian's car head-on. The car's hood crumpled, the seat belt locked up, and Brian's head and neck whipped back violently.

Paramedics extracted Brian from the wreckage and transported him to a nearby hospital using the paddles of life twice to get his heart beating. One of the foremost neurosurgeons in the nation performed two operations on the day of the crash. The prognosis was grim. His spinal cord was badly bruised, and two of his vertebrae were shattered. The doctor shared with family and friends that, with injuries this extensive, the odds were 95% that he would continue life as a quadriplegic.

Why did this happen to Brian? It seemed like such a careless and senseless act made by the driver who hit our son. Was she on her phone, distracted, changing the channel on her radio? Our son's life was forever altered by her actions. All his hopes and dreams for the future were taken from him.

After two weeks in the hospital, Brian was transferred to the Rehabilitation Institute of Chicago for two months of intensive physical therapy. As Brian worked hard and pressed himself every day to improve a little more, he was interviewed by two different news channels, two newspapers, and one magazine. One interviewer asked him, "What is it that keeps you going?" He replied, "Faith in God, family, and friends."

Brian came home from the rehab institute on weekends. During one of those weekends, a bouquet of flowers was delivered to our home. The envelope was addressed to Brian, so I put them on the table in front of him as he sat in his wheelchair. I opened the card, and the short message read, "Hoping you are getting better." It was from the lady who had crashed into Brian's car. I was angered that she sent the flowers, feeling she had no concept of what she had done to our son. I picked up the vase to toss the flowers out, not wanting them to be on our table. Brian looked up at me and said, "Mom, the flowers are beautiful. I have forgiven her, now you need to do the same."

I learned a valuable lesson from my son that day. Faith in God, family, and friends gives us strength for all that we may face in life, but we need to forgive. Life is too short to live with anger and bitterness.

Author's Note: We have known Brian and his family for more than twenty years.

The Lord's hand was on Brian from the first moments of the accident all the way through to the amazing outcome. Family and friends stood in faith on Brian's behalf countless times, through many months. The Lord heard and answered our cries.

During months of painful, demanding rehabilitation, Brian did everything his doctors and therapists demanded. He was relentless in his courage and tireless in his determination to get better. His attitude was positive, and his goal was fixed: to get back on his feet. It also helped to have the love and support of an amazing young woman, his wife-to-be, Brytne, at his side.

A year after the doctors had given the family the grim diagnosis that Brian would likely be paralyzed from the neck down, he returned to the pitcher's mound with his college baseball team! Brian's faithfulness, tenderness of heart, and forgiveness surely helped him heal—not to mention his fierce determination, self-discipline, and a wonderful team of doctors and therapists. What could have resulted in a lifetime of pain, God turned around and used for good. Brian and his doctors did all that they could, and then God did all that they couldn't. Brian's recovery, against all odds, is a miracle and testimony of the power of prayer and God's relentless grace and healing power.

Brian's testimony of God's faithfulness has touched and inspired thousands. Today, Brian and Brytne have two happy, healthy boys and live in the suburbs of Chicago.

The Brain & The Mind

"The mind creates the brain."
–Dr. Jeffrey Schwartz

Consider the brain. The average brain weighs around three pounds, about 2% to 3% of an average person's total body weight. Yet it uses 20% to 30% of the calories we consume and 20% of the body's blood flow. A newborn baby is born with about 100 billion nerve cells. According to Dr. Jeffrey Schwartz, "These 100 billion neurons connect to as many as 100,000 other neurons through connections called synapses. As the brain develops into adulthood, it hosts about 100 trillion synapses, or electrical connections." Understanding these synaptic connections, UCLA researchers recently announced that the brain "has more than 100 times the computational capacity than was previously thought." This amount of computational power inside every one of us rivals the largest, most expensive supercomputers on Earth. That is a lot of brain power!

Here's the process: we connect with the world primarily through our five senses: sight, hearing, taste, smell, and touch. Our sensory receptors transmit information to the brain, specifically, to the "thalamus, which acts as a neural receiver and transmitter station." It receives and processes information and then sends it to the cerebral cortex, which helps us understand the information (hot or cold, bitter or sweet, safety or danger, etc.). The cerebral cortex can also trigger an emotional response (fear, calmness, anger, etc.). The thalamus then creates a chemical response in the endocrine system by producing hormones. Then, the little "amygdala deals with the most passionate perceptual emotions" (fight or flight responses).

While these processes are running, the hippocampus creates and accesses memories and motivation. These memories are stored as proteins in structures called axons and dendrites, which look like branches on a tree. "Proteins are made and used to grow new branches to hold our thoughts" during a process called protein synthesis.

Memory

Every thought, experience, reflection, and prayer is stored as a memory along with its associated emotion. Dr. Caroline Leaf is not only a world-renowned neuroscientist and researcher, she is also a Christian and prolific author. "Every time we build a memory, we activate emotions," writes Dr. Leaf. When we recall a specific event, we also experience the emotion of it all over again. This is powerful. In this way, we experience events twice (or more): once when we live it and then again when we remember it. With pleasant memories, we repeat the pleasure. With negative emotions, like unforgiveness, the associated "toxic" memories produce stress, and the hormonal responses associated with it hammer our systems all over again.

Our memory of offense still remains. It is stored as proteins in axons and dendrites in our brains. However, the act of forgiveness summons the emotion attached to the memory and neutralizes the negative emotion. It removes the emotion of its power to control us. Forgiving others doesn't erase our memories, but it does take the sting out of them. This is why God tells us to "cast our cares upon Him." The act of casting our grudges and wrongs upon God sets us free. We are free to live our lives in happier and healthier ways. Free of poison. Free of the trap of the enemy who would seek to hold us captive to the debt that actually claims us.

When someone wrongs us and we forgive them, the memory of the event will remain for awhile, but the hurt will lessen over time. We may recall the event in the months to come, but it lacks the power to anger us or make us bitter. The root of bitterness is removed. Being freed from its power frees us to love and live on.

Neuroplasticity: The Renewing of Our Minds

"Whatever you think about most will grow."
–Dr. Caroline Leaf

Just twenty years ago, neuroscientists thought that "the brain was structurally immutable by early childhood and that its functions and abilities were programmed by genes." We were taught that the brain was merely an input/output device. We now know that is not so. Indeed, to the contrary, the brain changes, forming new connections that become stronger with use. "The neural electrician is not restricted to working with existing wiring; we now know he can run whole new cables through the brain." This neural mapping and remapping is a direct result of conscious thought and is always in operation.

Neuroplasticity is the term used to describe how our brains alter themselves based on our thoughts, actions, feelings, and experiences. Neuroplasticity simply means that the brain is forever changing, moment by moment of every day. As Dr. Caroline Leaf wrote, "Every time we make a decision, we change the physical structure of our brain." Dr. Schwartz reinforced this point, saying, "The life we live, in other words, shapes the brain we develop. Our brain is marked by the life we lead and retains the footprints of the experiences we have had and the behaviors we have engaged in." Schwartz goes on to say, "We know that the formation of new synapses as a result of the growth of existing axons or dendrites is involved in the remodeling of circuits and cortical remapping."

In 1997, neuroscientists discovered that learning and experience actually create new neurons, a process called neurogenesis. Nobel laureate Eric Kandel examined how changes in the environment caused nerve cells to change. It caused new extensions called axons that send information to parts of the brain. The reverse also happens. According to Kandel, "Unused synapses grow weaker and weaker until they are able to carry signals no better than a frayed string between two tin cans in the old game of telephone." In fact, every change in the environment—internal and external—causes a rearrangement of cellular activity and growth.

Dr. Schwartz spent twenty-five years studying the mind, brain, and behavior. His research included a body of work involving OCD patients and teaching them how to learn. He found that focus, will, and intentionality could cause the brain to rewire, enabling his patients to learn. He discovered that even learning disabilities have to yield to the mind when it is determined to get something done. By teaching patients alternate ways of thinking and acting, the brain gradually rewired itself accordingly to accomplish the task.

Similarly, Schwartz wrote about research with people who had suffered strokes. Using a technique called "Constraint-Induced Therapy," researchers discovered that our brains are capable of changing themselves as situations require. Physical therapists worked with patients who had suffered strokes on their right sides, resulting in no mobility of their right arms. They bound up the left arm and gave the patients tasks to perform. Unable to move their good arm, patients' brains began to remap their neural pathways and re-stimulate their damaged right arms. This cortical remapping yielded astonishing results, as the brain revealed its adaptability to the environment when the situation demanded it as a result of focused human will.

Our minds are in control of our brains and our bodies. While we cannot control the events and circumstances of life, we can control our reactions to those events. When we think, pray, and build thoughts, they become physical substances in our brains. Dr. Leaf puts it this way: "Whatever you think about the most will grow." Here's the thing. Forgiveness grows healthy dendrites and axons in the brain, while unforgiveness makes these neural branches brittle, dark, and dying.

Our thoughts, imagination, prayers, and choices change the structure of our brains. Neuroplasticity (the ability of the brain to change in response to thinking) can operate for us as well as against us because whatever we think about the most will grow. This applies to both the positive and negative ends of the spectrum. Dr. Leaf states, "Through our thoughts, we can be our own brain surgeons as we make choices that change the circuits in our brain. We are designed to do our own brain surgery." In this context, the mind has the power to change the brain.

Think about it. As we focus and pray and act in faith, we rewire our brains. When we believe God and meditate on His word, it takes up residence in us. As we read and remember scripture, that Word is stored in our memories as a protein construct. His Word becomes "flesh" and lives inside us. We are not what we eat. We are what we think and believe in our hearts. Dr. Dawson Church asserts, "Our beliefs become our biology."

Furthermore, spiritual disciplines (daily prayer, reading, and memorization) become habit as they are repeated. Dr. Eric Kandel, Nobel Prize laureate in medicine, established that new behavior causes structural changes in the brain. The number of synaptic changes increases dramatically when that new behavior is introduced. However, unless that "initial experience was reinforced, the new circuitry in the brain decayed within a month!" Rehearsing things creates and firms up neural pathways. In other words, for a behavior to become a habit, it must be repeated. Dr. Leaf maintains that it takes 21 days for a new behavior to become a habit. This is important. Whenever we want to create a new habit, we need to give ourselves sufficient time for our brain to respond accordingly, which usually takes about three weeks.

Noted author Malcolm Gladwell writes that proficiency is the product of repetition. He suggests that it takes 10,000 repetitions to achieve proficiency. Practice makes perfect, indeed! If forgiving others becomes a daily discipline, think of the positive power of that. The mind and memory become fresh and alive. We enjoy peace and contentment.

As the Word of God is physically stored in us, Romans 12:2 comes to life; we are to "be transformed by the renewing of [our] mind[s]." Our minds are continually and radically being renewed as we get the Word in us. In this way, as our brain stores the Word, it becomes the Word. Dr. Leaf notes, "Bringing 'every thought captive' suddenly becomes a lot more important." See, we are what we think and believe in our hearts. This demands the questions: What are we storing in our minds, and what are we building up in our brains about God, about ourselves, and about each other? I am learning to be much more careful about what I store in my brain. Is it consistent with the Word of God? Does it build me up or tear me down? What do I put in front of my eyes? To whom am I listening?

Let's be clear about this. As our brains store the Word, it is alive and living in us. Literally. The Word of God takes up residence in our brains and dwells there in all its power. Consider this promise of Jesus: "*If you abide in* Me and My words abide in *you,* you will ask what *you* desire, and it shall be done for *you*." By reading (and memorizing) His words, they live, or abide, in us, and that promise is ours. Imagine.

Genes

A spiritual makeover will cause a genetic makeover, too.

Human beings have around 20,500 genes. Genes store information about our hereditary characteristics and tendencies. They work together, in concert with one another, and no single gene is responsible for much of anything. The idea of a single gene determining a particular characteristic makes for exciting headlines but lousy science. There is no single cancer gene or fat gene, for example. "Very few human processes are turned on or off by a single gene. Most processes require many genes acting together," writes Dr. Church.

As Dr. Leaf notes, "It is interesting that we control much of our genetic expression through our thinking." Geneticists and neuroscientists now believe that our genes are controlled, to a great degree, by what we think, feel, and say. This field of genetic research is called epigenetics. At its most basic level, epigenetics is the study of how our thoughts impact our physical brains, bodies, mental health, and spiritual development. What we think and say affects our health.

Dr. Caroline Leaf says that epigenetics is actually an ancient science that we find throughout the Bible. She writes, "Spiritually, this is the enactment of Deuteronomy 30:19, which says, 'I have set before you life and death, blessing and cursing; therefore choose life, that both you and your descendants may live.'" Our choices impact the generations that follow us.

Epigenetics clearly shows that what we think, say, pray, and do affects our genes. That genetic instruction is then passed onto the next generation and thereafter. Whether that result is healthy or unhealthy, it gets passed down.

The key ingredient in activating this genetic code is our minds. As Dr. Church says, "Our internal environment (prayer life, spiritual life, emotions, thoughts) as well as our external environment (food, toxins, relationships) activate our genes." Dr. Daniel Amen agrees, saying, "Our habits and emotions can impact our biology so deeply that it causes changes in the genes that are transmitted to the next several generations. It is through epigenetics that immediate environmental factors like diet, stress, toxins, and prenatal nutrition can affect the genes that are passed to our offspring."

We should know, however, that the sins of our parents create a predisposition, not a certain destiny. We are not responsible for ancestral decisions. However, as Dr. Church states, "We are responsible, however, to be aware of them, evaluate those predispositions, and choose to eliminate them." But even as positive, healthy, spiritual changes can occur in our genetic makeup, so can the opposite. Depression, anxiety, stress, and many other afflictions can be passed down epigenetically generation after generation. The effects don't last for only one generation. They can last for many. "Iniquities of the fathers" can indeed be passed to the third and fourth generations.

If there are some genetic qualities we don't want to inherit for ourselves or our children, there is good news. Our inherited genes do not necessarily determine our destiny. Dr. Caroline Leaf suggests that "75% to 98% of genetic expression is controlled by our thought life." This is a profound change from what earlier scientists believed. According to Dr. Church, "In reality, genes contribute to our characteristics but do not determine them. Genes account for 35% of longevity while lifestyles, diet, and environmental factors account for 65%. Beliefs, prayers, thoughts, intentions, and faith often correlate much more strongly with our health, longevity, and happiness than our genes do." If this is true, we are not victims of our biology. We control our thoughts, intentions, and faith. Therefore, to a great extent, we control how our genes express themselves in our lives. This is powerful and liberating news.

Our bodies are continually responding to what we do, think, and say. Every minute, about one million of our cells die. An equal number are also born. We have an opportunity every minute to send new epigenetic signals to the cells that are just getting born. As scripture says, "God's mercies are new every morning" (Lamentations 3:23). Every single molecule in our brain is replaced every two months. Every single cell in our bodies is replaced every seven years. A spiritual makeover causes a genetic makeover, too!

Given that we are constantly changing and editing our own genetic instructions, we need to guard our thoughts and words most carefully. Imagine if we recorded every word we spoke. What instructions would we hear ourselves giving? Put another way, the very words we think and speak impact our health and our future in profound ways. Not to mention the fact that our children's futures are on the line. If we change the "words of our mouths and the meditations of our hearts," we change our biology. We change our destinies. We become the masters of our lives instead of victims.

What then shall we think? The spiritual insights from Philippians 4:8 take on new meaning: "Finally, brethren, whatsoever things are true, whatsoever things are honest, whatsoever things are just, whatsoever things are pure, whatsoever things are lovely, whatsoever things are of good report; if there be any virtue, and if there be any praise, think on these things." Thinking on these things helps activate the genes consistent with these qualities.

Heart & Soul

Forgiveness does more than heal our bodies. It heals our souls.

Dr. Richard Restak writes, "Change your thoughts and you change your brain; change your brain and you change your feelings." Neural pathways are being created with every thought and feeling and spoken word. In Biblical terms, "As a man thinks in his heart, so he is" (Proverbs 23:7).

The heart is the seat of emotion and feeling. Neuroscientists have discovered that the heart actually has a cluster of nerves attached to it that acts as a second "brain." People who make decisions kinesthetically, based on their gut feelings, are using this ability. "Your heart is in constant communication with your brain and the rest of your body, checking the accuracy and integrity of your thought life. As you are about to make a decision, your heart pops in a quiet word of advice," says Dr. Caroline Leaf. "It is well worth listening to this advice, because when you listen to your heart, it secretes ANF (atrial natriuretic factor)—a hormone produced by the heart that regulates blood pressure and can give you a feeling of peace."

Often, we cannot control what the world sends our way. We are all confronted with the unexpected. But neuroscience says that we can control our reactions to it. Our immediate thoughts are triggered by the amygdala, which delivers a fight or flight reflexive reaction. But more thoughtful and deliberate responses are determined by our higher brain functions located in the cerebral cortex and anterior cingulate. If we take a little time to think about our responses instead of making knee-jerk reactions, we find that raw emotion yields to thoughtfulness and reason. But we need to give our brains time to kick in. For this reason, anger management counselors teach prisoners the technique of "taking a minute" before reacting. In this way, we can *choose* how and when we respond to provocation.

Finally, the will is the chairman of the board of the soul. It rules our decision-making process. Until that voice is heard, there is no action. God has made each of us with a will and freedom to act and choose. It is with the will that we choose to love, to fear, to believe, and to act. Our will takes input from our minds and hearts, but it makes the final decision. In the end, nothing happens until the will steps in and acts. And we control our own will. In the final analysis, our actions, thoughts, and reactions are determined by *us*, not external events. That freedom of choice is what makes forgiveness happen or not. And we always have the choice to forgive or not.

Charleston – Amazing Grace

In the summer of 2015, Ferguson, Missouri, erupted into racial violence and death. Same for Baltimore. Then, one Tuesday night in Charleston, South Carolina, the hate-fueled Dylann Roof shot and killed nine innocent people at a Bible study in the Mission Bible Church. The crime was horrific, but the response of the church was amazing. At Roof's sentencing hearing, several families of the victims expressed forgiveness for the murderer. Despite their pain, loss, and grief, they summoned the grace of God to extend forgiveness to him.

Suddenly, the community had peace and calm. The nation saw the grace of God and caught her breath. Our eyes and hearts swelled, sensing something special, something loving, something divine in that moment. There would be no riots in Charleston. No looting or arson or deaths like in Ferguson and Baltimore. The church had stood up in the power of grace and forgiveness. The church had confronted the hatred and evil of the enemy. And the church had won.

CHAPTER 3

Forgiveness
& Spirit

"We are not humans having a spiritual experience. We are spiritual beings having a human experience."
–Pierre Teilhard de Chardin

ON A SPIRITUAL LEVEL, forgiveness is the centerpiece of the Christian experience. God's forgiveness makes us whole and returns us to right standing with Him. His forgiveness of us is the center of salvation, and everything depends on that act. So completely so, that with his last breaths on the cross, Jesus interceded for us: "Father, forgive them; for they know not what they do." Jesus gave up everything, including His life, that we might be forgiven. He died that we might live. Jesus' forgiveness at the point of death is a picture of how we are to live, no matter how great the price.

Jesus teaches us two things: that we need to ask the Father's forgiveness and to forgive others daily. God's forgiveness cleanses us from the effects of our misdeeds. He unfastens us spiritually from sin and its consequences. And the consequences of sin are death. However, if we confess our sins to Jesus, "He is faithful and just to forgive us our sins and cleanse us from all unrighteousness." Because of Jesus' work on the cross, we can live free from the price of sin. Forgiveness restores us to wholeness with God and with each other. Having received from Him, we freely give to others. This needs to be our daily activity. It is the way we need to live.

Thinking About God

Dr. Henry Stapp says, "There is no stronger influence on human values than man's belief about his relationship to the power that shapes the universe." Something happens to us when we begin to think about God. Dr. Stapp writes:

> Something surprising happens in the brain. Neural activities begin to change. Different circuits become activated, while others become deactivated. New dendrites are formed, new synaptic connections are made, and the brain becomes more sensitive to subtle realms of experience. Perceptions alter, beliefs begin to change, and God becomes neurologically real.

In other words, when we contemplate God, He becomes real to us. This is why prayer, reflection, and worship are so important. As we approach God, He reveals Himself to us. His presence becomes noticeable. We sense His approach and nearness. His presence fills our senses with an excitement or quickening. We become alive to God. The two disciples experienced this very thing on the road to Emmaus, exclaiming, "Didn't our heart burn within us?" They knew they were in the presence of the Lord. We can have the same experience today through the presence and movement of the Holy Spirit within us and among us.

Power of Prayer

The Bible says that the "effectual fervent prayer of a righteous man availeth much." Focused prayer is where the power lies. When we deliberately, intentionally, and purposefully focus on God, we change our brains. Neurological studies have shown that prayer increases blood flow to the brain, which also promotes healing. Brain surgeon Dr. David Levy says, "I have seen many positive results from prayer, and I'm convinced they go beyond any physical or psychological explanation. Not only have people's brains been healed, but many people have been released from shackles of bitterness, anger, and resentment, which can be the root cause of serious physical problems."

Things change when we pray. When people are prayed for, they get better faster. Larry Dossey wrote in *Prayer Is Good Medicine* that there are now 250 scientific studies demonstrating the link between prayer and health and longevity. Here are some documented highlights:

- Dr. David Levy, a practicing neurosurgeon in California, prays for his patients before he operates on them and has amazing results.
- Thomas Oxman at University of Texas Medical School examined the effects of social support and prayer on heart patients. He found that those who had both exhibited a mortality factor of one-seventh of those who did not. That's an 86% improvement over those who did not receive prayer.
- St. Luke's Medical Center in Chicago showed that patients who went to church regularly and had a strong faith were less likely to die and had stronger overall health.

- According to an Israeli study of 1,087 physicians, two-thirds of doctors in the country now believe prayer is important in medicine. Two-thirds said they encouraged their patients to pray. In a group of doctors composed of Christians (of all denominations) and Orthodox Jews, 80% believed that miracles happen today. 55% said they had seen miraculous recoveries in patients.

- Christian cardiologist Randolph Byrd designed a test in 1986 for 393 patients over a ten-month period in the coronary care unit at San Francisco General Hospital. The prayed-for patients had these results:

1. Five times less likely than the control group (not prayed for) to require antibiotics
2. Three times less likely to develop pulmonary edema (lungs filling with fluid)
3. None of the group required a ventilator (twelve of the control group did)
4. Fewer patients died

Given the scientific evidence, prayer ought to be our first response to illness, not our last.

Here is an amazing story about the power of prayer... Even retroactive prayer! Professor Leonard Leibovici took the files of 3,393 patients admitted for blood poisoning from 1990 to 1996 and separated these into two random piles: One pile would be prayed for, while the other would not be. The group that was prayed for was found to have a reduced rate of fevers, shorter hospital stays, and lower mortality rates. What was interesting is that the patients Leibovici prayed for had been discharged from the hospital ten years earlier! The healing power of prayer appears to work outside the normal constraints of time and space. As astonishing as this case is, it makes sense. After all,

God exists outside of time and space. He created everything that exists and knows the beginning from the end. It is more than our minds can grasp, but such is the great God of the universe.

Spiritual Warfare

Forgiveness is a spiritual battle. It's not really that much of a battle; we have the victory if we want it. If not, the enemy will seize that opening and drive us where we do not want to go, which is toward ruin and destruction. Paul speaks to this in 2 Corinthians, telling us that we need to forgive one another so that we don't "give Satan a foothold, for we are not ignorant of his devices." The enemy will use unforgiveness as a device to drive us into despair and resentment. We must recognize Satan as a defeated foe. Jesus stripped him of his authority and his kingdom. Jesus won the victory against the devil and invites us into that position of authority. We have every right to treat him as a trespasser in our lives and to actively, fearlessly, and emphatically resist him until he flees.

We have weapons against him. 2 Corinthians 10:4 tells us that our weapons are supernaturally powered by God. We are to resist the devil until he flees. We are to stand against him and, having done all, continue to stand. We have authority to act in Jesus' name against every scheme of the enemy. Finally, the blood of Jesus and the word of our own testimonies can overcome the forces of darkness. When we wield these weapons in the name of Jesus, make no mistake. We are formidable foes against the enemies of God. They must stand down before Him.

While we do not think of forgiveness as a spiritual weapon, the Word reminds us that when we forgive others, "we keep Satan from getting the advantage over us." (2 Corinthians 10:10). Keeping our hearts free from unforgiveness (despair, resentment, and bitterness) is critical to our ability to stand.

Fear

Unfortunately, our brains are more affected by negative than positive information. Fear is driven by negative thoughts that "trigger more than 1,400 physical and chemical responses. This activates more than 30 different hormones and neurotransmitters, throwing the body into a frantic state," according to Dr. Leaf. In the absence of reason, emotional reflexes rule our reactions, often to our detriment. Fear is an emotional response, and it is also spiritual bondage.

For several months in 2008, I found myself bound by fear concerning business and legal issues I was experiencing. I was bound by the spirit of fear. Whenever I thought about the issues and the effect it could have on me and my family's future, I was paralyzed. Fear gnawed at my mind. Worry consumed me. There was no relief. I couldn't sleep. Anxiety overwhelmed me, and I had no peace, only fear and dread. I couldn't shake it.

Then, one morning while I was reading the Bible, it occurred to me that Jesus repeatedly teaches us to not be afraid, saying, "Don't be afraid, do not fear, fear not!" Jesus tells us, "Let not your heart be troubled, neither let it be afraid." Then, it occurred to me that Jesus wouldn't command me to do something that I couldn't do. If He was telling me to do something, then I *must* be able to do it. He was telling me not to be afraid. Suddenly, I understood that fear was a choice. I could *choose* to be afraid or not.

Twenty-seven times in the New Testament, Jesus tells us not to be afraid. Once or twice is important. Three times is imperative. Twenty-seven times is yelling. There is good reason for Him to warn us. First, fear interrupts our communion with Him through the Holy Spirit. Second, it debilitates us, distracting us from the opportunities and blessings of the day. It's impossible to be grateful when we are fearful. Fear paralyzes us, rendering us fallen on the battlefield before the fight has even been engaged. Finally, and perhaps the most important reason of all, 2 Timothy 1:7 tells us that "God does not give us the spirit of fear, but power, love, and a sound mind."

Fear is not from God—it is from the enemy. And if comes from the enemy, I don't want it in my life. Satan comes "to kill, steal, and destroy." Spiritually, being in a state of fear, anxiety, or unforgiveness opens the door to the enemy, who then has a foothold in my life to attack. It puts me and my family at risk.

Once I realized that being afraid was a choice, I prayed and told the Lord that I would obey Him. I decided not to fear. I would give the whole matter to Him in accordance with 1 Peter 5:7: "casting all your cares upon Him, because he cares for you." Immediately, I was delivered. The bonds that had held me were broken. I was instantly relieved and delivered of the spirit of fear. I could breathe again. Fear had vanished the moment I was obedient to His word.

In the days that followed, I found it helpful to recall these verses, reminding me of His faithfulness:

"I can do all things through Christ..." Philippians 4:13

"For with God nothing shall be impossible." Luke 1:37

"Thanks be to God who always leads us to triumph in Christ..." 2 Corinthians 2:14

Fear is an automatic, emotional response to a threatening situation. But, as Richard Restak states, "We are not slaves to the automatic responses mediated by our amygdala and other components of our brain's emotional circuits." We have a choice. Our choice is to cast off fear. Cast our cares unto the Lord. Resist the enemy. Stand in healing and wholeness. And enter into the rest of the Lord, who eagerly awaits our presence even as we seek His.

Deliverance

Deliverance and spiritual warfare have the goal of "releasing a person's will so that he can respond directly to the Lord and receive the help that God has for him." Think about this. When Satan oppresses someone, he binds them from being able to exercise their free will. According to L. Morrill Burke, "The nature of evil is the impulse to power over others." Put another way, the nature of evil is the desire to control and manipulate others. This is how Satan works. Jesus came to earth "to destroy the works of the devil" and to set the captives free. Deliverance is the manifestation of God destroying the enemy's stranglehold on a person's life. God moves in power so that the captive can regain free will.

Frank and Ida Hammond were very effective and experienced ministers of deliverance. In *Pigs in the Parlor*, Frank Hammond writes, "Mr. A had been tormented for twelve years, requiring extensive treatment and medical care for unforgiveness he had been carrying around concerning a serious injustice done by a medical orderly. It was explained to him that he could not be delivered from his spiritual tormentors (according to Matthew 18:32–35) until he had decided, chosen, and willed to forgive that man. He sat for five minutes trying to decide whether he would hold onto his hatred for that man. It took all the strength he could muster, but finally, he said, 'With the help of Jesus, I forgive that man.' This act of will paved the way for a complete deliverance."

Hammond shares a prayer of deliverance used to break the bonds of the enemy:

Lord Jesus Christ, I believe you died on the cross for my sins and rose again from the dead. You redeemed me by your blood and I belong to you, and I want to live for you.

I confess all my sins—known and unknown—I'm sorry for them all. I renounce them all.

I forgive all others as I want you to forgive me. Forgive me now and cleanse me with your blood. I thank you for the blood of Jesus Christ which cleanses me now from all sin. And I come to you as my deliverer. You know my special needs—the thing that binds, that torments, that defiles: that evil spirit, that unclean spirit—I claim the promise of your word. 'Whosoever calls on the name of the Lord shall be delivered.' I call upon you now. In the name of the Lord Jesus Christ, deliver me and set me free. Satan, I renounce you and all your works. I loose myself from you, in the name of Jesus, and I command you to leave me right now, in Jesus' name. Amen!

Chapter 4

Forgiving Others

Forgiving others changes <u>us</u>, it changes <u>our</u> hearts.

FORGIVENESS IS FOR everyone in our lives. Everyone needs forgiveness because no one is perfect, not one. We are just imperfect in different ways. And forgiveness instantly releases the power of love and heals and restores us to the right relationship with our heavenly Father.

Jesus teaches us one more step. In Matthew 5, He teaches us to bless our enemies and to pray for those who hurt us. This is a critical element. To recover fully from a hurtful experience and to grow spiritually, we need to take this step. But sometimes, it is easier said than done. It is easy to love those who love us, but that is not what Jesus is saying. He says, *"But I say to you, love your enemies, bless those who curse you, do good to those who hate you, and pray for those who spitefully use you and persecute you"* (Matthew 5:44). This is a direct challenge to all believers to forgive hateful, cursing, mean, confrontational people in our lives. Here's the thing: Jesus is serious.

Years ago, I was in a difficult situation at work. I reported to a man who was tyrannical to everyone in the office, frequently losing his temper, storming about, and swearing and lashing out at whoever was in his path of rage. This happened daily, it seemed. He knew I was a believer, but that didn't matter to him. His outbursts were insulting, demeaning, and foul. I can put up with a fair amount verbally, but hearing the word "Jesus" used as an expletive creates a strong physical reaction in me that is nearly unbearable.

For months, I carried around bitterness toward that man, and I despised him. I begged God to let me quit that job. He didn't. I knew I was supposed to forgive him; I had read Matthew. I knew the deal, but I didn't want to forgive. I was justified in my unforgiveness. This guy was mean and hurtful and miserable. I even got cute about it. I could bring myself to pray for his wife because it must have been awful to be married to such a jerk. I could pray for his kids in a kind of sympathetic sorrow. But I would not forgive him.

Then, one day during prayer, the Father told me that He loved that guy. That Jesus died for him. And in that moment, He allowed me to see the man through Jesus' eyes. His love toward the man flooded over me. It broke me. I wept and wept under the power of love God had for him. I was completely convicted about judging him and the hardness of my own heart. So I repented, I forgave him openly and earnestly, and began to pray *for* him. I honestly and emphatically began to intercede for his life and family and soul before the throne of grace. I implored God to forgive him, to bless him, to cover him and his family with grace, mercy, and protection. I prayed for his life on his behalf. In that moment, I was *for* him, too. "Love your enemies, bless them that curse you" had never felt so alive and real to me. It lifted my spirit and broke the hold of unforgiveness that was on my life. I was also out from under a shadow the enemy intended to use against me. It was done. I was free.

In Ephesians, the Holy Spirit writes, "let all bitterness and wrath and anger and clamor and slander be put away from you, along with all malice. Be kind to one another, tenderhearted, forgiving each other, just as God in Christ also has forgiven you." Believers often wonder, "What is the call of God on my life?" The Lord calls us to be kind and tender and forgiving. Forgiveness is a great place to start.

Annie's Story

Were you Daddy's little girl or his all-time favorite fishing buddy? Was he a provider, funny, kind, steady, firm, diligent, a protector, faithful? Was he your 'safe place'? Some descriptions of my father are: alcoholic, drug addict, bipolar, gifted, jokester, Christian, schizophrenic, abusive, and unfaithful. I simply call him lost! As you can imagine, the word "father" held nothing beautiful or nostalgic in my mind.

I don't have many memories from my early childhood, but one thing I do remember is having dart gun wars in our living room. We would flip our couches over and strategically make forts out of the cushions. I LOVED this game, and my Dad was always the initiator of all the fun. We would laugh, chase, and giggle with excitement. But in a moment, it would all change. He would go from cool, calm, and collected to angry rage in a blink. It would catch us off guard and, quickly, fear would set in. We never knew when he would turn the switch. I remember being fearful when my mom would leave us home alone with Dad. I didn't feel safe. I didn't trust him.

When I was a little older, the fear of my dad's behavior turned into anger. I had no idea how to honor, respect, and love him. I remember feeling disgusted when I would see my friends hug, kiss, and say, "I love you" to their fathers. Seriously, I couldn't physically understand that kind of relationship. In junior high, I remember being so angry at my dad that I planned to run away from home, but I felt I couldn't leave because I needed to protect my mom. In reality, I'm sure my mom didn't need my protection, but in my young mind, that's truly what I believed. For years, I prayed that my dad would leave us alone, that they would just divorce. I couldn't understand why my mom stayed married to a man who had given her every possible valid reason to leave. Finally, it happened. My parents divorced in 1997. Strangely enough, I reacted differently than I had expected I would. I wept in front of the whole family, asking them not to follow through. To this day, I still don't fully understand my reaction.

The divorce did bring peace, but it also brought out an unexpected side of my dad. He completely released his parental duties and instead tried to include me in his dark, unhealthy practices. He offered me drugs and alcohol and discussed personal things with me that were beyond inappropriate. The following few years brought more of the same: drug addiction, recovery, broken marriages and relationships, changing jobs, repentance, AA, alcohol addiction, and on and on.

Shortly after my husband, Josh, and I were married, my dad was living in a crack house in Chicago. He had made some statements that made my sister and me believe that he was going to commit suicide. So Josh and I drove into a terribly bad neighborhood in Chicago and brought him back to our home. Again, you would think that I would have written him off then, but I didn't want to. I hoped that he could be set free. I wanted to hope that maybe, someday, I could have a real father! He agreed to the rules of our home and followed those rules... for a while. Unfortunately, the dreaded cycle appeared yet again, and he brought drugs into our home, so he could no longer stay with us. We placed him in the Teen Challenge recovery program. From that time on, I believe he has avoided drug and alcohol use, but the behavioral cycle continues. He has moved from state to state and caused confusion and hurt wherever he went. Once in a great while, he has called to check in, but that's all. This is the extent of my relationship with my dad.

In 1998, my mom met someone special. Of course, I was a bit suspicious the first time he walked up to our house in a suit with a big bouquet of flowers for their first date. So, I made sure to be the first one he met just so I could make sure I didn't see an ounce of my dad in him. I can spot people like my dad a mile away! He seemed nice enough, so I let her go... like I had any choice in the matter! Little did I know that the Lord had sent that man to not only love, protect, and provide for my mother but to SHOW me what it means to have a TRUE father. It didn't happen overnight, but over time, I learned how to trust, how to follow, how to receive love, and even how to say "I love you!" As silly as it sounds, it was extremely hard to even say those words to anyone. He showed me that if I had a need, he would provide for it. If I were ever lost, he would use every resource to find me. If I were hurt, he would do whatever he could to heal me. He would lay down his life for me... FOR ME. He was a window into heaven, a glimpse of my heavenly Father's PERFECT love for me. He taught me, and is continuing to teach me, so much, and I am forever grateful that the Lord allowed me to know a father's love here, on this earth. As I experienced this type of love from him, strangely enough, it helped me show more mercy and grace to my dad.

So, I had to make a tough decision. I had to decide whether or not I could forgive my dad. Could I forgive him for how he treated me as a child? Could I forgive him for the incredible damage he caused? Could I forgive him for choosing everything else over me? Could I forgive him for the scars he left me to deal with as an adult? And the biggest question of all, could I forgive him as he CONTINUES to make the same mistakes? Forgiveness without true reconciliation— is it even possible? Purely by the grace of my Lord Jesus Christ, I say that it is possible. How do I know? Because I am living it every day.

In Matthew 18, Peter came to Jesus and asked Him, "Lord, how many times could my brother sin against me and I forgive him? As many as seven times?" Jesus replied, "I tell you, not as many as seven times but 70 times seven!" Jesus offers my dad the same forgiveness He offered me when I was lost, held together by my scars and drowning in sin. So, I CHOOSE to offer that forgiveness to my dad today and every day. I CHOOSE to HOPE for reconciliation. I CHOOSE to BELIEVE for freedom and peace for my Dad. Because I have experienced the true love of an earthly father as well as the true love of my Heavenly Father, I have been given the freedom to walk in forgiveness. And I CHOOSE forgiveness.

Forgive & Forget

There is no mystery here. The love we have for God and for each other comes straight from Him. "We love Him because He first loved us." All kindness, longing, and benevolence come from Him. It is no wonder that the forgiveness and forgetfulness we need also come from Him. God is a forgiver and a forgetter.

So, who are we to hang onto our sins when the Father has forgiven and forgotten them? Are we more righteous than God? Are we greater than the King of Kings? Of course not. We must resist the temptation to clutch onto other people's trespasses, believing they owe us something. The very thing we hold onto, we will soon discover, is holding onto us.

God forgives and forgets our sins. Psalm 103 says, "As far as the east is from the west so far has He removed our transgressions from us." And in Hebrews, God says, "Their sins and their lawless deeds I will remember no more." With forgiveness, He includes forgetfulness. God forgives and forgets every wrong, never to be brought up again. He calls on us to follow His lead and enter into divine amnesia as we forgive and forget.

Why does God expect us to forget other people's wrongs? There are two reasons: 1. That's what *He* does, and He is our highest and best example, and 2. That's what love does. 1 Corinthians 13:5 says that "love keeps no record of wrongs." Love pardons the offense and discards the record of it, never to be seen or heard from again.

So, do we lose our memory of the offense? No, but forgiveness takes the "sting" out of it. Forgiveness strips the offense of its ability to hurt, control, and embitter us. The act of forgiveness allows us to rise above the meanness of the offense and continue on with our lives.

Sometimes, it seems impossible to forget. Forgiveness can seem more like a process than an event, especially when someone has hurt us multiple times and we recall repeated offenses, time after time. In these cases, the need for forgiveness is greater, not less, and is never impossible. There is always grace to forgive. Grace waits patiently for our decision, our free choice to forgive. And when we do, bitterness and wrath must bow its knee before the healing power of forgiveness and grace.

I have found that I need to be a frequent forgiver. I need to ask myself daily if there is anything from anyone that has crept unaware into my heart. Life happens. We get crossed or offended. It is important to quickly dispose of those offenses before they can take root. For me, this requires daily discipline.

There is another important point that needs to be made. Forgiving others does not mean that we give them permission to continue their bad behavior. We will forgive them, but they are not entitled to continue to hurt us. If we are involved with a tormentor, we need to distance ourselves or remove ourselves entirely from that relationship. Wisdom should prevail in such cases. We can forgive others, sure, but that does not mean we are their scapegoats or doormats. In such cases, we should prayerfully consider what needs to be done in the interests of safety and protection for all involved. Sometimes, that requires removing ourselves from the situation.

Jesus & Peter: A Picture of Forgiveness and Reconciliation

Soon after I was saved, the Lord gave me a vision. I saw forgiveness come alive in John 21:3 as Peter struggled with his betrayal and failings. I could hear the waves slapping the side of the boat and hear the stillness of that morning. Peter had disavowed Jesus at a critical juncture, just before His mock trial and crucifixion. So much had happened in those few days. Peter had not seen the Lord since he had told people, "I never knew him." He had lied, abandoning his Lord and best friend. Peter had saved his own skin. The grief and guilt and shame weighed heavily upon him that morning...

"Simon Peter said to them, 'I am going fishing.' They said to him, 'We are going with you also.' They went out and immediately got into the boat, and that night they caught nothing. But when the morning had now come, Jesus stood on the shore; yet the disciples did not know that it was Jesus." KJV John 21:3–4

Morning broke wide on the horizon where the sky met the sea. The waves slapped softly against the boat as it drifted in the morning swells. As Peter stared fixedly into the distance, his thoughts were far removed. For the first time in a long time, he felt utterly alone.

Jesus had been his best friend, closer even than his brother. They had eaten, laughed, prayed, and lived together, side by side, for three years. Now, he was gone. Peter was adrift without the Lord. His heart ached with the emptiness.

Someone called out from shore... The other guys cast a net over the side of the boat. John turned to him and said, "It is the Lord." Immediately, Peter threw on his fishing cloak and dove into the water, swimming fast. With great splashing strokes, he swam toward shore.

Jesus rose and strode powerfully into the waves to meet his friend. Peter burst out of the water and threw himself into the arms of the Lord. Hugging each other tightly, Peter sobbed with inconsolable sorrow as tears streamed down their faces.

Forgiveness had been offered and accepted.

Justice

Forgiveness does not seek to justify the crime or the offence; it seeks to heal the soul.

I understand that simply forgiving others for what they have done seems unfair. After all, damage was done, and we've been hurt. We don't want to forgive the other person. We want justice or vengeance. If we've been hurt, getting even seems fair. And it feels a lot better than, "Oh, I forgive him." After all, forgiveness is not fairness. The other guy hurt us. How about some justice? How about some fairness?

People commit heinous offenses against each other, which are difficult to forgive. These situations require supernatural doses of forgiveness. God Himself grants us that forgiving power, the grace to forgive. It must be so. There is nothing inside of us that wants to forgive. In our heart of hearts, if we are being honest, most of us prefer the ancient remedy of "an eye for an eye and a tooth for a tooth." We want justice, vengeance, and fairness. As Dr. David Levy puts it, "Forgiveness is giving up my right to hurt someone who hurt me."

I am a justice guy. I like to see the weak and vulnerable protected and predators punished. The bad guys don't deserve grace and mercy. They deserve what's coming to them. Unless, of course, I am the one who messed up. Then, I'm glad God has patience, grace, and mercy.

Dr. Luskin quotes Frederick Buechner:

Of the seven deadly sins, anger is possibly the most fun. To lick your wounds, to smack your lips over grievances long past, to roll over your tongue the prospect of bitter confrontations still to come, to savor to the last toothsome morsel both the pain you are given and the pain you are giving back—in many ways, it is a feast fit for a king. The chief drawback is what you are wolfing down is yourself. The skeleton at the feast is you.

And there's no doubt: Forgiveness is not justice. It isn't fairness. It doesn't decide who's right or wrong. To forgive means to release a just claim on another. It is exemplified most powerfully by Jesus on the cross. He did not deserve crucifixion; he had done nothing worthy of death—even Pontius Pilate said so. There was nothing just or fair about killing Him. Nonetheless, He did not demand fairness or justice. Christ had already died to himself and was alive to God. He asked the Father for one thing: to forgive those who had trespassed against Him. He is our best and highest example.

Forgiveness is not about justice. It's about healing and peace and wholeness.

A Story About Supernatural Grace

Recently, a couple approached me with an account of God's supernatural intervention of forgiveness and healing. They were made aware that their young son had been secretly molested by an older cousin. They were angered, shocked, and mortified. This horrific attack on their child left them very angry and hurt. They discussed involving the police and estrangement from that part of the family. They prayed. They prayed over their son, asking for protection and healing and no damaging effects to him emotionally or psychologically. They also prayed for the offender.

Then, they confronted the cousin. He confessed what he had done and was repentant, tearfully asking for forgiveness. Still, the damage was done. They weighed the options, considering further action. Then, in a moment of supernatural grace, the father spoke to the nephew, saying, "We forgive you. You no longer have our trust; that will have to be earned, but we forgive you for what you have done." In an instant, forgiveness was complete. The Holy Spirit and grace flooded everyone, cleansing hearts, refreshing spirits, and washing away the hurt and bitterness.

In the father's words, "The pain was over. The weight was off our shoulders. Anger had put us both in bondage, but the power of forgiveness freed us. I can't explain it, but when we forgave him, everything changed."

Needless to say, the parents were vigilant and guarded in future dealings with the cousin, but the relationship was preserved. They were all reconciled in supernatural grace.

"It was a God thing," says the dad. "Only His grace made this possible. Our son is fine, by the way. He has suffered no lasting effects from the attack. It was the Holy Spirit that compelled us to forgive him. Only He could have made this happen. There was no other way."

CHAPTER 5

Forgiving Ourselves

Forgiveness does not change the past, but it does change the present and the future.

FORGIVING OURSELVES IS one of the most difficult things in life, for everyone—believers or not. We can believe that God forgives us our sins, but some of us cannot forgive ourselves. Although God has forgiven our failures, we carry them around like a bag of rocks. Millions of Christians live under the burden of condemnation from past sins.

A common stumbling block among believers is a feeling of unworthiness. We tend to drag around guilt, shame, and regret like they are old friends. In reality, those burdens weigh us down and drag us back into the swamp. When we repented from sin, we turned and headed in a new direction, away from failings and falling, away from sin, and toward the calling of God on our lives. One of my favorite verses is Philippians 3:13–14: "...this one thing I do, forgetting those things which are behind and reaching forward to those things which are ahead, I press toward the goal for the prize of the upward call of God in Christ Jesus."

According to Romans 8:1, "There is therefore now *no condemnation* to those who are in Christ Jesus, who do not walk according to the flesh, but according to the Spirit." This means that believers do not have to live under condemnation. We are not under the heel of past sins. God sees us "hidden in Christ." God sees us as He sees His own Son: blameless, worthy, righteous. If we would lay ahold of this truth and step into our inheritance in Christ, we would more fully enjoy our lives and easily fulfill our destinies.

The Word says that Jesus endured the humiliation, shame, and pain of the cross "for the joy that was set before Him." What was that joy? What joy could possibly have been worth the pain of choking for air and bleeding to death? *Us.* His love for us filled His heart with joy. If Jesus says we are worthy of His sacrifice, then we are.

Jesus died for our sins. He died for all of our sins: past, present, and future. How could He die for our future sins, you ask? As Joseph Prince teaches, when Jesus died 2,000 years ago, all of our sins were in the future! He died "once for all." Not a few, not some, but all. Yesterday, today, and tomorrow are bound up and forgiven by his sacrifice on the cross, once and for all. We are free of our past and the bondage of sin and death forever. His sacrifice was sufficient. In fact, Jesus' sacrifice was more than enough to cover all the sins of the world.

We are called to life: a life of forgiveness, of right relationship with God, of kindness and tenderness toward each other. It makes us stronger, happier, peaceful, joyful, and whole. It is always helpful to check our own hearts. Are we tender-hearted toward each other? Do we suffer wrongs gladly? Do we forgive quickly? These are keys to victorious living.

We have an enemy. One of his tactics is to remind us of our failures, inadequacies, and sins. If he can succeed in that, he can keep us captive and conquered by shame, discouragement, and self-loathing. As Joseph Prince says, he tries to make us *sin*-conscious instead of *Christ*-conscious. His weapons against us are designed to take our focus off God. If the enemy can succeed in that, he can bring us down. You can be assured that the enemy is fully aware of this maneuver.

When he reminds us of our past offenses, we must immediately call to mind God's love for us, Jesus' sacrifice that paid the penalty for all of our sins, and the continual cleansing fountain of God's forgiveness. We must remind ourselves that there "is no condemnation in Christ Jesus" for us. Jesus is "faithful and just to forgive us of our sins and to cleanse us from all unrighteousness." We must proclaim this truth and stand on this firm foundation.

However, some people insist on clinging onto those past sins and memories. And the enemy loves to whisper in our ears to drag us back under his control. The nature of evil is the impulse to control other people. This is where the devil lives. He reminds us of our past sins under his mastership. He haunts us with feelings of regret and shame. He has discouraged millions from following their new nature, as new people, spiritually born again.

Here are two pieces of good news: Jesus came "to destroy the works of the devil." In the victory of His resurrection, Jesus restored His authority over everything Adam had forfeited. Jesus has been given "all authority in heaven and on earth" to act on our behalf. That assures us both victory and peace. Secondly, the past must no longer haunt us. God forgives and forgets. There is no longer a record of our wrongdoing in the Lord's eyes. It has been bought and paid for by the blood of Jesus. We are not to relive it, to revel in it, or to remain in it. What a powerful, liberating thing God does on our behalf.

In summary, we must forgive ourselves for our pasts. God did, and so must we. To do otherwise is to labor under a burden that is not ours to carry. It is to ignore what Jesus did for us on the cross and to frustrate grace. He took upon himself all of our burdens and sins, all of them, and His sacrifice is sufficient. Forgiving ourselves is really a call to understand our salvation. To miss this point is to miss everything.

God gives all of us grace. As the Lord has taught me, grace is the power to do that which is right.

CHAPTER 6

Forgiving God

Relationship with God

UNFORGIVENESS DAMAGES MORE than just our physical, mental, and emotional health, as harmful as that can be. It also affects our relationship with God. He is our Father with whom we should enjoy a loving relationship, but unforgiveness gets in the way. Pastor and author Kenneth Copeland says, "When you don't forgive, you can't hear." If we have been unforgiving toward others, it disrupts our relationship with God and prevents us from hearing Him. Conversely, researchers have found that forgiveness can "promote relational repair with God" and, "If you believe God loves you, it's an enormously protective factor."

Let's take it one step further. The trajectory of our Christian lives depends on two things: our view of God and God's view of us. As A.W. Tozer says, the right "view of God is the solution for 10,000 problems in life." Conversely, a poor view of God will result in 10,000 problems. God's view of us is well-established: the one who loved us enough to die for us died for us. Jesus showed the greatest love ever when "for the joy set before Him, He endured the cross." And "greater love has no one than this, than to lay down one's life for his friends."

But what about our view of God? What happens when our view of God gets clouded, even unintentionally, with blame or unforgiveness? Unforgiveness strains and tears at all of our relationships, including our relationship with our Father.

My Story

By 2008, I had been saved for several years and was used to getting my prayers answered. The Lord had blessed me in every way: financially, relationally, and spiritually. Things were going well, and I decided to start my own company. Of course, I had prayed about it but really hadn't heard anything definitive from heaven. In retrospect, that was a strategic error. I had interpreted silence from heaven as approval. But silence did not mean "yes." Neither did it mean "no." It was just silence. Undeterred, I plowed ahead and made several more poor decisions along the way. I ignored warning flags, checks in my spirit, that the Holy Spirit gave me. "After all," I thought, "I am experienced. I know what I am doing." Most importantly, I knew what *I* wanted. Now, there was a recipe for disaster. When I ignored warnings from the Holy Spirit, I entered a danger zone of the worst kind.

This is an example of pridefulness. It is incredibly dangerous when we become full of ourselves. When pride enthrones us, taking God's rightful place in our hearts, it blinds us. Looking back, it is very embarrassing that I fell into such an obvious and odious trap. I knew better.

Soon, I found myself and my young company headed into disaster. Faced with legal challenges and crushing financial issues, we were in deep trouble. To make matters worse, I had begun to blame God for not answering my prayers. Loren Toussaint's research shows that unforgiveness toward God causes high levels of stress and depression. I bore witness to this. I was stressed and depressed!

The fact is that I hadn't really noticed that I was harboring unforgiveness. It had snuck up on me. While I knew there was something out of place between God and me, I couldn't put a finger on it.

But secretly, I blamed Him for my failure. He could have rescued us, but He didn't. There was only silence from heaven. Deep down, I felt let down. I didn't really trust Him anymore. Not completely. Not like I once had. I was used to getting my prayers answered.

Over the years, the Lord had answered my pleas for mortgage money, successes at work, for things to work out in my favor. He had answered those cries. The Lord had given me an amazing list of answered prayers and victories. And I expected Him to continue to deliver. I expected Him to perform on cue. However, as Bill Johnson said, "If God is your servant, you will become frustrated and disappointed. However, if you are God's servant, you will continually be amazed and delighted." I found myself frustrated and disappointed.

For five years afterward, I harbored lingering questions, doubts, and unforgiveness in my heart toward God. Then, one day, after I had been teaching about forgiveness, it occurred to me that I was guilty of the very thing I had been warning others against. I needed to forgive God. So I dropped to my knees and told Father that I forgave him. In that moment, I heard Him chuckle. Then I started to chuckle. Then, I wept tears of relief.

From deep within me, there arose a powerful release, freedom from that burden I had been carrying around. For years, it had shaded my feelings toward Father. It had begun to poison me spiritually. It had begun to turn me against God. That simple act of "forgiving God" released me from the thralls of bitterness that threatened my relationship with Him, that stole my peace. The shackles of unforgiveness were broken. I was free. "Forgiving God" repaired my relationship with my heavenly Father.

God brings only blessings and love and life and goodness to every one of us. He does not inflict us with sickness and death and destruction. It is the enemy, not Father, who comes to "kill, steal, and destroy." We often get it mixed up. It's a bad rap. The Lord comes to destroy the work of the enemy and to give us life more abundantly. If we suffer destruction, death, or loss, the first place we need to look is the enemy's camp. And if the devil does worm his way into our lives, it's because we left the door open. We have the authority, given to us by Jesus, to boot him out and shut the door.

Whatever has happened, whatever the pain and loss and hurt and sorrow, we have to know that God is a good Father, the very best. There is no other like Him. He is tenderhearted, kind, wise, and compassionate. Forgive God if you need to. Do not allow the shadows of evil to overtake your spirit. Cry out to God, tell Him you forgive Him (as ridiculous as that might sound), and see for yourself the liberating, refreshing, and restorative power of spiritual forgiveness. Then, go after the enemy. Bind Satan and his minions, assault his camp, and reclaim what he has stolen (Joel 2:25). Sometimes, we just need to "warrior up" and go after the enemy of our souls. Jesus has given us the authority and power to reclaim what the enemy has stolen. But it is up to us to take the victory to him.

The Good Father

Some people think it's weird that God speaks to me. I have to say, it seems normal to me. After all, He *is* my Father. It would be weird if He *didn't* speak to me. What kind of father would never speak to his son? He tells me things I need to know. He corrects, teaches, and encourages me. Sometimes, He just breaks into my day to tell me He loves me and that I am not alone. God is a really good Father, the very best.

In preparation for writing *Forgiving God*, He told me, "Millions of Christians have unforgiveness in their hearts toward me. Tell them I am a good father." God gets blamed for lots of stuff, all of it unjustly. The devil is the god of this world for now. He owns the blame and responsibility for poverty, disease, famine, and disasters. And we do our share of messing things up. Too many times, we blame God instead of taking responsibility ourselves.

Consider our heavenly Father. He has never hurt us. There are those who misquote the Bible and say, "Well, God gives and takes away. He gives and takes away." There is not an ounce of truth in that statement. That superstitious nonsense arose out of misunderstanding the Bible and the nature of God. The only thing God has ever taken from me was pain, disappointment, despair, and addiction. The only thing He has broken were the chains that bound me. And the only things he ever destroyed in my life were the works of the devil: hopelessness, addiction, poverty, selfishness, lying, so much more. It is a long list.

"But," some people say, "what about old Job? God sure took a lot away from him!" The enemy, not God, destroyed Job's family and stole his possessions. That's what Satan does: kill, steal, and destroy. For the record, God had placed a supernatural hedge of protection around Job, but *Job opened himself* up to attack. When Job chose fear and dread in his life, when he accepted what the devil had for him, he left a gate wide open through that hedge of protection. Where does the Bible say that Job did that? Job 3:25 says, "For the thing I *greatly feared* has come upon me, and *what I dreaded* has happened to me." God had not given Job the spirit of fear, the enemy did (2 Timothy 1). So, what's the point? Instead of guarding his peace and trusting in God and resisting the enemy, Job accepted the enemy's fear into his mind and heart. The minute he did that, the enemy pounced. The whole disaster was Job's fault, not God's.

Jesus came to destroy the works of the enemy and to give us a more abundant life (John 10:10). He is deserving of our love and obedience, not our blame. And as we turn our affection toward Him, we find Him present. If you don't know this kind of intimacy, take a moment right now and ask Jesus to give you His presence. He will. It is His promise. In fact, the Lord desires to be with us even more than we want Him! The Father gives the Holy Spirit to those who ask. And the Holy Spirit never seeks His own fame or reputation or glory. The Spirit of God always serves to reveal Jesus.

If you haven't heard from your heavenly Father lately, I would urge you to talk with Him and turn your affections toward Him. As we draw near to Him, He draws near to us. But it is up to us to make the first move. He is always a perfect gentleman and never forces Himself on anyone.

His love and affection for us know no bounds. He orders and reorders time and space and resources to meet our every need. He lavishes us with grace and mercy and love. He protects us and lifts us up when we are beaten down. His is the touch that always heals. His love is inestimable. His grace knows no limits. His truth is indomitable. His affection has no end. His ways are unsearchable. His wisdom has no equal. His continual desire is for our wholeness and because of Him and in Him, we are.

The Prodigal Son: A Portrait of Forgiveness and Unforgiveness

The story of the prodigal son is a powerful and touching picture of repentance, forgiveness, and reconciliation. Less commonly discussed, though, is the painful example of unforgiveness, as portrayed by the older son. Let's take a look at the story which Luke tells in chapter fifteen:

"Jesus continued: There was a man who had two sons. The younger one said to his father, 'Father, give me my share of the estate.' So he divided his property between them.

Not long after that, the younger son got together all he had, set off for a distant country, and there squandered his wealth in wild living. After he had spent everything, there was a severe famine in that whole country, and he began to be in need. So he went and hired himself out to a citizen of that country, who sent him to his fields to feed pigs. He longed to fill his stomach with the pods that the pigs were eating, but no one gave him anything.

When he came to his senses, he said, 'How many of my father's hired servants have food to spare, and here I am starving to death! I will set out and go back to my father and say to him: Father, I have sinned against heaven and against you. I am no longer worthy to be called your son; make me like one of your hired servants.' So he got up and went to his father.

But while he was still a long way off, his father saw him and was filled with compassion for him; he ran to his son, threw his arms around him, and kissed him. And the son said unto him, 'Father, I have sinned against heaven, and in thy sight, and am no more worthy to be called thy son.'

But the father said to his servants, 'Bring forth the best robe, and put it on him; and put a ring on his hand, and shoes on his feet.'"

The father saw his son "a great way off." How did that happen? Because he was watching for him. Although no word had come from the boy and he had been presumed dead, the father had not given up watching for him, hoping against hope. Day after day, the father had searched the horizon. And, then, finally, he saw that familiar shape appear in the distance. At the first sight of the boy, the father broke into a run.

In our lives, even as we make a decision to turn to God, He is already in full stride headed toward us. He is already arranging and rearranging the strands of time and resources and relationships to meet our needs. So great is His love, God is in a headlong run toward us.

The wayward son was well aware of his failures. He had asked for and received all of his inheritance and had spent it partying with his friends. It is interesting that some friends last only as long as the money holds out. When the good times are gone, they are too. The prodigal son had rehearsed what he needed to say, probably all the way home. As soon as his father reached him, he began his repentance speech. "Father, I have sinned against you and am no longer worthy to be...." he said. But the father was not interested in his speech. You see, there are two kinds of repentance: words and deeds. When the son had turned for home, he also had changed the direction of his life. His actions spoke louder than words. His feet testified of the repentance of his heart. Nothing—not hunger, filth, fatigue, sickness—was going to stop him from reaching his dad.

The son was not worthy of such a homecoming, as his older brother would soon point out. But forgiveness is not based on worthiness. It is based on the Father's indescribable, incomprehensible, unchanging love. Love and compassion, not judgment and condemnation, met the prodigal son.

Many of us have sons, daughters, nieces, nephews, or grandchildren who are away from God. When worried families ask me what to do about "prodigal children," I tell them, "Get a pair of binoculars and running shoes." Even now, those sons and daughters are "coming to themselves," making a decision to head for home. When they are in sight, we will run and embrace them. We will greet them with forgiveness and cover them with love. There will be time enough to clean up the mess later. But in that moment, we'll receive them back into the family with grace, mercy, and forgiveness, just as our heavenly Father restores us.

For those who await that special day, we must pray. We have spiritual authority for those we love. Spiritually, our prayers clear the air above their heads. That covering provides a space free of the clamor and confusion of the enemy, so they can make a clear-headed decision. It provides our kids with a space of grace against a relentless enemy who seeks only to "kill, steal, and destroy."

So, we will be more relentless, more emphatic, and more powerful than the enemy. We will wrap our spiritual authority, woven of love, around them like a cloak, protecting them from harm. We will stand as intercessors against the enemy before the throne of grace. In the name of Jesus, we command the devil and his crowd to stand down. In the name of Jesus, I rebuke the enemy from my family and bind him in the name of Jesus. Where does this spiritual authority come from? It is given to us by Jesus. We have His permission to use His name in Matthew 28, Luke 10:19, and a variety of other places. I will never forget when God told me, "You have authority for all of those you love." It explains why Jesus operated with such far-reaching authority and power: He loved the whole world.

The story continues:

"Meanwhile, the older son was in the field. When he came near the house, he heard music and dancing. So he called one of the servants and asked him what was going on. 'Your brother has come,' he replied, 'and your father has killed the fattened calf because he has him back safe and sound.'

The older brother became angry and refused to go in. So his father went out and pleaded with him. But he answered his father, 'Look! All these years I've been slaving for you and never disobeyed your orders. Yet you never gave me even a young goat so I could celebrate with my friends. But when this son of yours who has squandered your property with prostitutes comes home, you kill the fattened calf for him!'

'My son,' the father said, 'you are always with me, and everything I have is yours. But we had to celebrate and be glad, because this brother of yours was dead and is alive again; he was lost and is found.'"

In contrast to his brother, the older son had become resentful. Under Jewish tradition, the older brother received twice as much as the younger; he received 2/3 of the estate, all that his father had left. Despite this, he had grown bitter about the whole deal. He treated his father roughly, complaining disrespectfully, "Look! All these years I have been slaving for you..." His father responded gently, saying, "You are always with me, and everything I have is yours..." But the older brother would have none of it. He even refused to acknowledge his relationship with his own brother, referring to him as "this son of yours." The older brother stubbornly refused to accept his brother back. Unforgiveness was doing its dark and deadly work.

We don't know how the story finally ended. We are left with the closing scene of the older brother unwilling to forgive, angry and alone. Which of the two sons was out of relationship with the father? What a price for choosing an unforgiving spirit.

CHAPTER 7

Unforgiveness

Unforgiveness is like drinking poison
and waiting for the other guy to die.

–Anonymous

THERE IS GOOD REASON that God tells us to forgive others. Scripture refers to unforgiveness as "bitterness." The Greek word is "pikra," which means poison or bitterness. Unforgiveness is poison to us, gradually killing us, spiritually and physically. The Bible says, "the root of bitterness has defiled many" and leads to death. Unforgiveness hardens the heart. It can be fatal and is a danger. We must be vigilant to make sure bitterness finds no root in us. Once poison is in the root, it relentlessly feeds until it kills the whole plant.

The renowned neurosurgeon Dr. David Levy writes, "Bitterness is like a disease. Releasing bitterness can dramatically help the underlying causes of many physical ailments, often more than any pill or procedure."

Unforgiveness: Health Effects

Unforgiveness also has serious negative health effects in older adults. These include higher heart rate, blood pressure stress, and heart disease. Dr. Toussaint found that the risk of "arteriosclerosis, hypertension, angina, tachycardia, and other cardiovascular ailments" are increased in people who did not forgive. Frank Hammond writes, "The consequence of allowing the root of bitterness (resentment, unforgiveness, recalling the hurts, anger, hate, and retaliation) to remain is physical infirmities such as migraine headaches, indigestion, ulcers, colitis, and arthritis. It should come as no surprise that some arthritis is clearly a result of prolonged bitterness." Just to be clear, these are serious physical conditions resulting from a spiritual condition. The correlations and consequences of our emotional and spiritual lives, of unforgiveness, are clear.

When we harbor unforgiveness toward someone, our bodies release cortisol into our bloodstream. Cortisol goes to work immediately, tensing our muscles, squeezing our lungs, and inhibiting blood flow to our brain, heart, and other vital organs. In addition, cortisol can also affect the immune system. Cortisol turns off the immune system after adrenaline has revved it up. High levels of cortisol accumulate from chronic stress. Stress is a killer.

Everett Worthington describes these health effects thus:

Unforgiveness can negatively affect health directly by creating stress responses that increase the risk of heart attack, stroke, and other cardiovascular illnesses.

Stress responses produce high levels of the neurohormone cortisol, which, in addition to affecting the cardiovascular system, has been connected to malfunctions of the reproductive system and of thinking and memory. Unforgiveness can also affect the peripheral nervous system, creating increased heart rate and blood pressure. It thus can damage the tender inside walls of arteries and veins. These damaged areas can collect fatty acids and other solid substances that float around in the blood and eventually harden the arteries and veins, leading to arteriosclerosis. Even more dangerous, chronic unforgiveness can keep the heart rate elevated, thus reducing heart rate variability, which has recently been linked to many increased risk factors for disease." from *The Power of Forgiveness*

Dr. Levy says, "Unforgiveness and resentment are the biggest blocks to healing. Unforgiveness is the number one thing that will prevent your immune system to get you on the track to healing."

Roy's Story

"My wife suffered severe postpartum depression after our first child was born. It was so debilitating, she was hardly able to function daily. In fact, she was so depressed at times that she didn't want to. So, when she became pregnant a second time, we talked it over and decided that an abortion was the best alternative. I went to the clinic with her, and it was done.

I immediately regretted the decision. No matter how I justified it, we had agreed to kill a baby. I became haunted by that thought. I was a murderer. To make matters worse, I became unfaithful to her. I then lived in the agony of being a murderer, adulterer, liar, and more. The accumulated burden of sin weighed on me every day. I felt condemnation and sadness and despair. I had no peace. Gradually, my health deteriorated. My intestinal tract got so bad I had to take medication just to eat.

Things were getting worse and worse when I finally spoke to a local pastor. He gave me a copy of "Forgiving God" and told me to read it. I did and found myself on my knees asking God to forgive me. Immediately, I felt relieved. The burden was lifted. God took all my sin from me in a moment. I was incredibly free from the weight I had been carrying around. It is an amazing thing when the Son of God forgives our sins.

God began to reveal His amazing creation all around me. As He showed me His creativity in nature, I marveled and drank in this revelation of Him! Everything changed for me. I saw God in the sunrise and in the beauty of the birds and everything that moved and grew and chirped. This realization of His greatness and glory and majesty excites and inspires me every day. But it started with healing. The healing power of His forgiveness. That's where it started for me.

I was asked, 'What did forgiveness do for me?' The answer is, 'It gave me God. And peace. It gave me peace.'"

Quid Pro Quo

Forgiving others releases God to forgive us.

God forgives us as we forgive others. This is hard-hitting, but we must not gloss it over or weaken it. It is too important. The Lord taught this truth to His disciples as a daily prayer saying, "Forgive us our debts as we forgive our debtors." This scripture has two connotations. God forgives us *like or in the same manner* as we forgive others. In other words, if we are forgiving to others, the Lord will be forgiving toward us. Secondly, God forgives us *when* we forgive others. His forgiveness *follows* our forgiveness. In both cases, the result is the same: if and when we forgive others, God forgives us.

Here is what He says:

Matthew 6:14 "For if you forgive men their trespasses, your Heavenly Father will also forgive you. But if you do not forgive men their trespasses, neither will your Father forgive yours."

Matthew 18:35 "So My heavenly Father also will do to you if each of you, from his heart, does not forgive his brother his trespasses."

Mark 11:26 "And whenever you stand praying, if you have anything against anyone, forgive him, that your Father in heaven may also forgive you your trespasses. But if you do not forgive, neither will your Father in heaven forgive your trespasses."

Luke 6:37 "Judge not, and you shall not be judged. Condemn not, and you shall not be condemned. Forgive, and you shall be forgiven."

Matthew 18:21 "Then Peter came to Him and said, 'Lord, how often shall my brother sin against me, and I forgive him? Up to seven times?' Jesus said to him, 'I do not say to you, up to seven times, but up to seventy times seven.'"

Peter asked a fair question, "How often should we forgive someone, seven times?" Jesus' response was not about the math. He made the point that we need to be continual forgivers, just as He is. Nurturing bitterness, resentment, hatred, unforgiveness, or plotting revenge and desiring to hurt others are all sin. And sin separates us from God. But the Word tells us that if we confess our sins to Jesus, "He is faithful and just to forgive us of our sins and cleanse us from all unrighteousness." God tells us in Mark 11:26 that if we have anything against anyone, we are to forgive our brother first, before we worship Him. Before we present ourselves to him in either praise or sacrifice, we must cleanse ourselves of unforgiveness. It's that serious.

This is strong stuff. But we need to know it is not okay for us to accept God's free gift of forgiveness and deny the same to others. God sees unforgiveness as spiritual hypocrisy, a double standard.

Please notice that repentance from the offending party is not mentioned here. While repentance is required for reconciliation, it is not required to forgive someone. After all, they may not know they have ever been forgiven by us. Forgiveness is for our benefit, not theirs. Some people get stuck on this point, stubbornly waiting for the transgressor to apologize before they forgive them. That is not what God is directing us to do. Nowhere in these five scriptures does He tell us to do that. On the contrary, we are to forgive unconditionally. "Well, if God requires repentance to forgive others, so should I," some might say. Besides the obvious point that we are not God, there is another. Forgiveness is not primarily about reconciliation with the offender. Forgiveness is concerned with the healing and wholeness of us who have been hurt.

And who are we to withhold forgiveness? If God is willing to forgive us our wrongs, who are we not to do the same for others? If God is willing to forgive us, who are we to deny others the same grace? Some might say, "Well, this guy deserves judgment." So do we. Are we better than God, more righteous? Are we so great that we have a special right to hold debts against those when the God of the universe freely forgives us our worst evils? It is a fearful thing to install ourselves on God's throne. Unforgiveness is pride. It puts us in God's place: rule maker, judge, and executioner. God resists the proud and gives grace to the humble. Forgiving others is an act of humility. And you can't out-humble God. He gave up His perfect son whom He loved to reconcile our evil with His righteousness.

Some of us hang onto an offense like an IOU. We refuse to give up our grudge until we receive an apology or admission or recompense. In the meantime, both parties are bound up in a relationship neither one wants. Our pride holds us hostage to the offender. Do we really want to be bound up with that other person? An apology may never come, but still, we clutch the IOU. Says Dr. Levy, "We think we're hurting the person, but actually, it's hurting our relationships, stealing joy from our very life." We end up paying the price twice: once when it happened and again when we carry it around with us. And all the time, it is hurting us. What a price.

There is another point: Those who are forgiven much are expected to forgive much. I have been forgiven much in my life. There is a debt I owe to be kind-hearted and quick to forgive others. Unforgiveness on my part is an offense to God.

Here's the thing: Our forgiveness of others releases God to forgive us. Conversely, harboring unforgiveness toward others constrains the hand of the Lord to forgive us, according to His word. I need His forgiveness daily. To forfeit that grace in order to carry a grudge makes absolutely no sense. "And be kind to one another, tenderhearted, forgiving one another, even as God in Christ *forgave* you." This is the way we need to live.

The Unforgiving Servant

Jesus was asked exactly what He meant by forgiving others. How many times should we forgive someone? Here's the parable (Matthew 18:21-35):

Then Peter came to Jesus and asked, "Lord, how many times shall I forgive my brother or sister who sins against me? Up to seven times?"

Please note, Jesus' response is not about the math. His point is that we must be frequent forgivers.

Jesus answered, "I tell you, not seven times, but seventy times seven. Therefore, the kingdom of heaven is like a king who wanted to settle accounts with his servants. As he began the settlement, a man who owed him ten thousand bags of gold was brought to him. Since he was not able to pay, the master ordered that he and his wife and his children and all that he had be sold to repay the debt.

At this the servant fell on his knees before him. 'Be patient with me,' he begged, 'and I will pay back everything.' The servant's master took pity on him, canceled the debt, and let him go.

But when that servant went out, he found one of his fellow servants who owed him a hundred silver coins. He grabbed him and began to choke him. 'Pay back what you owe me!' he demanded.

His fellow servant fell to his knees and begged him, 'Be patient with me, and I will pay it back.' But he refused. Instead, he went off and had the man thrown into prison until he could pay the debt. When the other servants saw what had happened, they were outraged and went and told their master everything that had happened.

Then the master called the servant in. 'You wicked servant,' he said, 'I canceled all that debt of yours because you begged me to. Shouldn't you have had mercy on your fellow servant just as I had on you?' In anger his master handed him over to the jailers to be tortured, until he should pay back all he owed.

This is how my heavenly Father will treat each of you unless you forgive your brother or sister from your heart."

What a sobering story. The debt that had been forgiven was reinstated, and the unforgiving servant was subjected to torment until the debt was paid in full. What a price!

The most common thing that will prevent a person from receiving deliverance is unforgiveness toward others. Hammond said, "Those who have any unforgiveness toward anyone else, dead or alive, cannot be delivered." Based on the parable of the unforgiving servant in Matthew, Hammond continued, "Unforgiveness puts us into the custody of tormenting spirits."

Furthermore, harboring unforgiveness gives the enemy a legal right to oppress us. This is a strong warning. And there is more: Jesus says in Matthew 6:14–15, "For if ye forgive men their trespasses, your heavenly father will also forgive you: But if you forgive not men their trespasses, neither will your Father forgive your trespasses." Holding a grudge against someone else puts us in danger spiritually. If we are unwilling to forgive other people, also made in the image of God, we put ourselves in peril that our heavenly Father will not forgive us our sins against Him. My understanding of this, based on the scriptures, seems pretty clear. If we need forgiveness, we need to forgive others.

Given our nature, it seems wise to make forgiveness of others a daily prayer.

Entanglement

Pastor and author Frank Hammond wrote, "In centuries past, the punishment for murder was to chain the murderer to his victim's body. He was forced to drag the dead body with him everywhere he went until it decayed and fell away of its own accord. What a dramatic illustration of what unforgiveness does to us. We are tied to the person we despise; we cannot get away from tormenting thoughts and emotions. What a price!"

When unforgiveness prevails, both parties become entangled in a relationship neither one wants. The unforgiven person is held in this broken relationship, and the unforgiving one is tormented. Dr. Leaf puts it this way: "If someone has hurt you and are 1,000 miles away, it's as if they are standing right in front of you. If you haven't forgiven them, you have allowed them access to your life." If we hold onto unforgiveness, we are connected to the very person who hurt us. Dr. Leaf says, "When we forgive them, we can remove them from our head."

Forgiveness disentangles us from our tormentor. This simple act breaks the invisible bond that connects us to that person. We are now free, and so are they—free to move on and heal emotionally and mentally.

Many of us look for justice. When does the tormentor pay the price for what he has done? What about revenge? The Word gives us that answer: "Beloved, never avenge yourselves, but leave the way open for [God's] wrath; for it is written, Vengeance is Mine, I will repay, says the Lord." They don't get off scot-free. When people mistreat us, we are to turn them over to Him. He has our back. He does not forget injustice to His children (2 Thessalonians 1:6).

In 1975, University of Maine English professor Dr. L. Morrill Burke lectured that "there is a certain tied-togetherness of things." Indeed, scientists are grappling with that very idea today. For example, how is it scientifically possible for a person to receive healing when they are far away from the person praying for them? Quantum physics begins to explain how this is possible by studying subatomic energy particles.

Quantum entanglement says that everything and everyone are in relationship with each other. Certain particles appear to move interconnectedly despite being separated by time and space. There is a tied-togetherness of things. This doesn't come as a complete surprise to believers. We know that God Himself exists outside the boundaries of time and space. He is the "beginning and the end." Time itself is in His hands.

In 2004, Leanna Standish of Bastyr University conducted an experiment with two people separated in distant rooms. Researchers flashed an image to the first person to see if an fMRI scanner detected brain activity in the second person. It did. There was a "significant correlation" observed between the two brains, although they were separated by distance. How was this possible?

Dean Radin, PhD designed a fascinating experiment. He had two people meditate together in a Faraday room, an electromagnetically shielded room designed to prevent any outside influences. After a while of being together, he separated the pair and placed them in separate shielded rooms about fifty feet away. He hooked both of them up to EEG machines and shone a light into the eyes of the first person at regular intervals.

Later, they examined the EEG readouts for both participants. The EEG machine of the first person recorded brain activity each time the light had been flashed in his eyes. Then they examined the readout for the second person and compared it to the first. The researchers found that, at the exact moment the light was shined at the first person, the brain of the second person also responded. How was this possible? They were separately shielded and consciously unaware of the stimulus of the other.

Dr. Radin concluded that humans are capable of connections with each other, even when electromagnetic signals, sounds, and visual cues are ruled out. Quantum physics postulates that subatomic energy particles are the agents of connectedness or entanglement. For our purposes, such research gives us a glimpse of understanding into how people can be connected with each other despite distance and time.

There is a universal connectedness. Einstein's "spooky actions at a distance" do exist. Any objects that have ever interacted continue to influence each other regardless of how far apart they are or how long ago the interaction occurred. "Events at the edge of the galaxy influence what happens at the edge of our garden." It seems that our world has a mysterious universal connectedness that goes beyond what we understand.

When we carry around unforgiveness, we remain in relationship with our tormentor, regardless of how long ago the incident happened or how far he or she is. Whether we are a thousand miles away or a foot away, according to quantum physics, we are bound together. Unilateral forgiveness severs that bond. Our prayer of forgiveness unfastens us from the offender. Choose to be whole again. Choose life for yourself and your heirs. Forgive.

Melody's Story

"I had been recently divorced and a single mom when a friend set me up on a blind date. It had been a difficult time, and my self-esteem was at an all-time low.

"For the first six or seven months, he treated me okay. I made him a part of our lives, introduced him to my daughter and our family. Then, he became more and more abusive.

He started treating me roughly, including hitting, slapping, pinning me. He began to beat me and even choked me once to the point of passing out. Partly, I blamed myself. I asked myself what I was doing to make him behave this way.

"I wanted to call for help, but he threatened my daughter. He said, 'If you tell anyone, remember, I know where your daughter goes to school. I know what time she gets out.' I was terrified. Finally, I got up the nerve to speak to a police officer. But he told me, 'Look, it's your word against his. Unless we witness the attack, there is nothing we can do. Those bruises don't prove that he did it.'

"Even the counselor I had seen was no help. He asked me what I had done to drive my husband 'to drink,' as if it was my fault. I was frightened and trapped. I felt like there was no one I could talk to. God was the only one. So, I prayed. I asked God to help me. A week later, that abusive man was arrested and sent to prison for four to five years. God answered my prayer.

"But over the years, I remained silent. Then, one day in church, the message was about forgiveness and the healing that it brought. I needed that. After all, I said to myself, I'm the one who's paying for it [the abuse] year after year, not him! So, I forgave him and all that he had done to me. Immediately, I felt the weight lift off me. I broke free.

"Then, recently, I heard that my church was going to start a victim services ministry. I had to tell my story. I just had to tell someone. So I wrote an email to my pastors and Jeff, telling them what had happened to me. But I wavered between sharing this secret or not. I wrote the email and then deleted it several times. But when I finally pressed 'send,' my tormentor's hold on me was broken. I was free like I hadn't been in years! Today, I feel so much better. I feel that sharing my private nightmare brought me closure and gave me my life back.

"I was asked what advice I would give someone who is facing what I went through. I would tell anyone in that situation: 'Don't let the past put you in an inner prison. There is help out there. Trust somebody. Tell somebody. And God is your advocate, you can tell Him anything. Get to church.'"

Concluding Thoughts

Forgiveness is for the undeserving. So is salvation. I am not deserving of God's pardon, yet I have it. If salvation was reserved for only those who are worthy, no one would qualify. Salvation is a free gift from God for the undeserving.

God forgives and saves everyone who asks because He is *for* everyone. No one is beyond His reach or His love. How do we know this? Because "God so loved the world that He sent His only begotten Son that whosoever believes in Him should not perish but have everlasting life." Jesus was "bruised for my transgressions and wounded for my iniquities." There is no more sacrifice to be made for my sin. It is already done. My failures and faults are hidden in Jesus, covered by the blood of His sacrificial death. God sent Jesus so that by believing in Him, we would become His sons and daughters. He extends His open hand filled with love, healing, and forgiveness to everyone who so believes.

God is the greatest forgiver of all time. The Bible tells us that God forgives us the moment we ask. He forgives and forgets all of our faults and failures in a divine display of love. And then, He invites us to do the same for each other, every day, for the rest of our lives.

In 2017, the Lord spoke to me, saying, "Jeffrey, I do not love you for what you do or don't do. I love you for who are." He told me I was His Son (Psalm 2). When that knowledge sank into my spirit, it changed my life. God taught me that when I fail, I do not come up short in His eyes. His opinion of me does not rise or fall based on my poor decisions. I may hurt myself and adversely affect my life, but I cannot hurt or affect Him in any way. He is entire and whole and perfect in and of Himself. He needs nothing and no one to make Him whole. He is who He is. And He is complete.

Furthermore, His love for me transcends my tendencies. His love is more than enough to cover my shortfalls. When I was saved, I became a child of God. He now looks at me differently than prior to that transformational relationship. He considers me family. This fact is obvious to some people but unbelievable to others; either way, it is critically important to grasp. We are hidden in Christ. In the eyes of the Father, Jesus' attributes are our attributes. And He has no faults or failures. This is liberating truth.

We do not have to labor to be "good enough." There is no such thing. Christ alone was sufficient to atone for my sins forever. Jesus was and forever will be more than enough. Through Him, we are all invited to become sons and daughters of God.

I pray that all of us who hold this book in our hands would ask for His forgiveness and invite Him into our hearts. That we would allow His truth to sink deeply into our spirits. That He would completely destroy the work of the enemy in our lives. And that the power of His love would radically transform our lives as we open up all He has for us. Sons and daughters are not broken, dismayed, or disowned. We are His and His alone. And "He shall perfect that which concerns us."

So, why do we forgive? We forgive because the grudge we are dragging around is killing us: spirit, soul, and body. And forgiveness is the power of God working in our lives. How do we forgive? We just do it. With an extra measure of grace from the Creator, we simply pray and tell the Lord that we forgive the offending party. Because forgiveness is God-breathed, it is also God-powered. When we tell Him that we forgive the offender for everything they did or said against us (whether we feel like it or not), the work is done. It's that simple. It's not a process; it's a supernatural event, an act of grace. Forgiveness is instant and just that powerful.

Once we take that step of faith to forgive, unforgiveness no longer has a hold on us. We are free from evil entanglements. Unforgiveness can no longer interfere with our relationships with God and others. Healed and whole, we can find our way home.

Salvation

Each of us is a three-part being: spirit, soul, and body. When we ask Jesus to forgive us of our sins and invite Him into our lives, our spirit is reborn. The Holy Spirit lives within us. The Holy Spirit comes to us for the primary purpose of revealing Jesus to us and in us. He never seeks His own glory or reputation, always that of the Lord.

In this way, we are born again. Our spirits come to life. Our souls begin a process of transformation, and we are changed from the inside out. The pace of this transformation lies in great measure with each of us. As we pursue God through reading His Word, praying, and engaging Him, we grow. As A. W. Tozer said, "Every man has exactly as much of God as he desires." How much of God we come to know and experience depends on us. There is no lack in Him. He is always ready with a full supply.

This amazing process of becoming alive in Him begins with a simple prayer:

"Lord Jesus, please forgive me of my sins. I invite you into my heart to be my Lord and Savior. Thank you for forgiving me, for loving me, and for saving me."

Forgiveness Discovery Tool

I have developed this simple tool for people who want to recall offenses that need to be forgiven. Sometimes, so much time has elapsed or the offense was so damaging that we have suppressed the memories.

"Lord, please bring to mind offenses I need to forgive in my life. Help me to recall those things that I need to release to you."

I was hurt when _____
_____. I remember [person's name] _____ and these episodes:

1. _____
   _____

2. _____
   _____

3. _____
   _____

Prayer of Forgiveness

Lord Jesus, in obedience of your example and your Word, I now forgive each and every person who has hurt me. Of my own free will, I forgive [name each person]. Lord, I bless each of these people and forgive them, just as you have forgiven me. I declare my love for them, I bless them, and I ask you to bless them, too.

As you have forgiven me, I also forgive myself, in the love of Jesus Christ. The curse of unforgiveness over me [and my family] is hereby broken, in the name of Jesus.

In Jesus' name I pray... Amen.

Endnotes

Introduction

1. *"root of bitterness"*
   NKJV. Hebrews 12:15.

Chapter 1: Forgive

2. Bradford, Thomas. (2018). Torah Class: *Rediscovering the Bible. New Testament Studies: Acts.* Retrieved from: http://torahclass.com

3. *"A man reaps what he sows."*
   NIV. Galatians 6:7.

Chapter 2: Forgiveness & Healing

4. *"Look on my affliction and my pain, and forgive all my sins."*
   NKJV. Psalm 25:18.

5. *"[God] forgives all your sins and heals all your diseases."*
   NKJV. Psalm 103:2.

6. *"Son, your sins are forgiven you."*
   NKJV. Mark 2:5.

7. *"Sickness is to the body what sin is to the soul."*
   Johnson, Bill. (2005). *The Supernatural Power of a Transformed Mind: Access to a Life of Miracles.*
   Shippensburg, PA: Destiny Image Publishers.

8. *"...our bodies release serotonin, dopamine and oxycontin into our bloodstream."*

    Leaf, Caroline. (2009). *The Gift in You.* p. 146.

    Southlake, Texas: Inprov, LTD.

9. *"...stronger immune systems, less physiological reactivity to stress..."*

    Toussaint, Loren; Worthington, Everett, Jr. & Williams, David. (2015). *Forgiveness and Health.* p. 33.

    New York, NY: Springer.

10. *"...improving the central nervous system..."*

    Worthington, Everett Jr. & Scherer, M. (2004). Forgiveness is an emotion-focused coping strategy that can reduce health risks and promote health resilience: Theory, review, and hypothesis. *Psychology and Health.* 19, 385-405.

11. *"Cardiovascular health improved by forgiveness"*

    Toussaint, Loren & Cheadle, Alyssa. *"Unforgiveness and the Broken Heart: Unforgiving Tendencies, Problems Due to Unforgiveness, and 12-month Prevalence of Cardiovascular Health Conditions."* Religion and Psychology. (2009). Nova Science Publishers, Inc.

12. *"At the University of Wisconsin, a study involving thirty-six Vietnam vets..."*

    Church, Dawson, PhD. (2014). The Genie in Your Genes. p. 182.

    Santa Rosa, CA: Energy Psychology Press.

13. *"...only recently discovered importance of forgiveness."*

    Toussaint, Loren & Williams, David. "National Survey Results for Protestant, Catholic, and Nonreligious Experiences of Seeking Forgiveness and of Forgiveness of Self, of Others, and by God." *Journal of Psychology and Christianity,* Vol. 27, No. 2. 120-130. (2008).

14. *"...enhance mental health and reduce depression."*
     Toussaint, Loren.; Marshall, Justin & Williams, David.
     "Prospective Associations between Religiousness/
     Spirituality and Depression and Mediating Effects of
     Forgiveness in a Nationally Representative Sample
     of United States Adults." *Depression Research and
     Treatment*. Vol. 2012, Article ID 267820. (2012).

15. *"...forgiveness is protective for our minds and bodies..."*
     Ibid.

16. *"...connections between forgiveness and higher self
     esteem, lower anxiety, and depression."*
     Toussaint, Loren; Worthington, Everett, Jr. & Williams,
     David. (2015). *Forgiveness and Health*. p. 25
     New York, NY: Springer.

17. *"...positive results in psychological and emotional
     well-being."*
     Luskin, Fred. (2010). *Forgive For Good: A Proven
     Prescription for Health and Happiness*. p. 78.
     New York, NY: HarperCollins.

The Brain & the Mind

18. *"The mind creates the brain."*
     Schwartz, Jeffrey & Begley, Sharon. (2002). *The Mind &
     The Brain*. p. 364.
     New York, NY: HarperCollins Publishers.

19. *"...2%-3% of body weight... 20%-30% calories..."*
     Amen, Daniel. (2015). *Change Your Brain, Change Your
     Life*. p. 27.
     New York, NY: Harmony Books.

20. *"...100 billion nerve cells..."*
     Schwartz, Jeffrey & Begley, Sharon. (2002). *The Mind
     & The Brain*. p. 111. New York, NY: HarperCollins
     Publishers.

21. *"These 100 billion neurons connect to 100,000 other neurons..."*
Ibid. p. 366.

22. *"...UCLA researchers recently announced..."*
Gordon, Dan (ed.). Brain is 10 times more active than previously measured, UCLA researchers find. UCLA Newsroom. March 9, 2017.
Retrieved from: http://newsroom.ucla.edu/releases/ucla-research-upend-long-held-belief-about-how-neurons-communicate

23. *"...the thalamus which acts as a neural receiver..."*
Leaf, Caroline. (2009). *Who Switched Off My Brain?* p. 51. Southlake, Texas: Inprov, LTD.

24. *"...the amygdala deals with passionate responses..."*
Leaf, Caroline. (2009). *Who Switched Off My Brain?* p. 54. Southlake, Texas: Inprov, LTD.

25. *"proteins are made and used..."*
Ibid. p. 60.

Memory

26. *"Every time we build a memory, we activate emotions."*
Leaf, Caroline. (2009). *Who Switched Off My Brain?* p. 55. Southlake, Texas: Inprov, LTD.

27. *"'toxic' memories produce stress..."*
Ibid. p. 56.

28. *"...casting all your care upon Him, for He cares for you."*
NKJV. 1 Peter 5:7.

Neuroplasticity: The Renewing of Our Minds

29. *"Whatever you think about most will grow."*
Leaf, Caroline. (2013). *Switch On Your Brain.* p. 63 Grand Rapids, MI: Baker Books.

30. *"...the brain was structurally immutable..."*

Schwartz, Jeffrey & Begley, Sharon. (2002). *The Mind & The Brain.* p. 366.

New York, NY: HarperCollins Publishers.

31. *"The neural electrician..."*

Schwartz, Jeffrey & Begley, Sharon. (2002). *The Mind & The Brain.* p. 253

New York, NY: HarperCollins Publishers.

32. *"Neuroplasticity is the term..."*

Leaf, Caroline. (2013). *Switch On Your Brain.* p. 22.

Grand Rapids, MI: Baker Books.

33. *"Every time we make a decision...we change the physical structure of the brain."*

Leaf, Caroline. (2009). Who Switched Off My Brain? p. 61.

Southlake, Texas: Inprov, LTD.

34. *"The life we live... shapes the brain."*

Schwartz, Jeffrey & Begley, Sharon. (2002). *The Mind & The Brain.* p. 179.

New York, NY: HarperCollins Publishers.

35. *"Our brain is marked by the life we live..."*

Ibid. p. 212.

36. *"We know that the formation of new synapses..."*

Ibid. p. 252.

37. *"The Nobel laureate Eric Kandel, examined how changes..."*

Newberg, Andrew & Waldman, Mark. (2009). *How God Changes Your Brain: Breakthrough Findings from a Leading Neuroscientist.* p. 15.

New York, NY: Ballantine Books.

38. *"Unused synapses grow weaker..."*

Schwartz, Jeffrey & Begley, Sharon. (2002). *The Mind & The Brain.* p. 366.

New York, NY: HarperCollins Publishers.

39. *"Every change in the environment causes a rearrangement..."*
    Ibid. p. 253.

40. *"Dr. Schwartz spent twenty-five years studying the mind, brain, and behavior."*
    Ibid. p. 253.

41. *"He found that focus, will, and intentionality could cause rewiring of the brain..."*
    Ibid. p. 257

42. *"using a technique called Constraint-Induced Therapy"*
    Ibid. p. 194.

43. *"This cortical remapping yielded astonishing results..."*
    Ibid. 195.

44. *"Whatever you think about most will grow."*
    Leaf, Caroline. (2013). *Switch On Your Brain.* p. 63
    Grand Rapids, MI: Baker Books.

45. *"Through our thoughts, we can be our own brain surgeons..."*
    Leaf, Caroline. (2013). *Switch On Your Brain.* p. 55.
    Grand Rapids, MI: Baker Books.

46. *"Our beliefs become biology."*
    Church, Dawson. (2014). *The Genie in Your Genes.* p. 37.
    Santa Rosa, CA: Energy Psychology Press.

47. *"Furthermore, spiritual disciplines become habit as they are repeated."*
    Ibid. p. 99.

48. *"However, unless that 'initial experience was reinforced..."*
    Ibid. p. 99.

49. *"...it takes 21 days for a new behavior to become a habit."*
    Leaf, Caroline. (2013). *Switch On Your Brain.* p. 147.
    Grand Rapids, MI: Baker Books.

50. Gladwell, Malcolm. (2011). *Outliers – The Story of Success.*
    New York, NY: Hatchette Book Group.

51. *"...be transformed according to the renewing of your mind."*
    NKJV. Romans 12:2.

52. *"...bringing every thought captive."*
    NKJV. 2 Corinthians 10:5.

53. *"If you abide in me, and My words abide in you, you will ask what you desire, and it shall be done for you."*
    NKJV. John 15:7.

Genes

54. *"Human beings have about 20,500 genes."*
    NIH: National Human Genome Research Institute. (2016). *An Overview of the Human Genome Project.* Retrieved From: https://www.genome.gov/12011238/an-overview-of-the-human-genome-project/

55. *"Very few human processes are turned on or off..."*
    Church, Dawson. (2014). *The Genie in Your Genes.* p. 81.
    Santa Rosa, CA: Energy Psychology Press.

56. *"...genetic expression through our thinking..."*
    Leaf, Caroline. (2013). *Switch On Your Brain.* p. 128.
    Grand Rapids, MI: Baker Books.

57. *"...epigenetics is actually an ancient science..."*
    Leaf, Caroline. (2013). *Switch On Your Brain.* p. 14.
    Grand Rapids, MI: Baker Books.

58. *"I have set before you life and death..."*
    NKJV. Deuteronomy 30:19

59. *"Our choices impact the generations that follow us."*
    NKJV. Numbers 14:18.

60. *"Our internal environment...activate our genes."*
Church, Dawson. (2014). *The Genie in Your Genes.* p.30.
Santa Rosa, CA: Energy Psychology Press.

61. *"Our habits and emotions can impact our biology so deeply..."*
Amen, Daniel. (2015). *Change Your Brain, Change Your Life.*
New York, NY: Harmony Books.

62. *"We are responsible, however, to be aware of them, evaluate those predispositions..."*
Church, Dawson. (2014). *The Genie in Your Genes.*
Santa Rosa, CA: Energy Psychology Press.

63. *"Depression, anxiety and other forms of stress can be passed down epigenetically..."*
Ibid. p. 260.

64. *"Iniquities of the fathers"*
NKJV. Numbers 14:18.

65. *"In reality, genes contribute to our characteristics but do not determine them."*
Church, Dawson. (2014). *The Genie in Your Genes.* p. 32.
Santa Rosa, CA: Energy Psychology Press.

66. *"75%-98% of genetic expression is controlled by our thought life."*
Leaf, Caroline. (2013). *Switch On Your Brain.* p. 33.
Grand Rapids, MI: Baker Books.

67. *"Genes can influence our characteristics but do not determine them."*
Church, Dawson. (2014). *The Genie in Your Genes.* p. 32.
Santa Rosa, CA: Energy Psychology Press.

68. *"Genes account for 35% of longevity while lifestyles, diet, and environmental factors..."*
Ibid. p.32.

69. *"Beliefs, prayers, thoughts, intentions, and faith often correlate much more strongly..."*
Ibid. p.32.

70. *"Every minute, about one million of our cells die."*
Ibid. p. 259.

71. *"They [God's mercies] are new every morning."*
NKJV. Lamentations 3:23

72. *"Let the words of my mouth and the meditation of my heart be acceptable in Your sight, O Lord, my strength and my redeemer."*
NKJV. Psalm 19:4.

73. *"Finally, brethren, whatever things are true, whatever things are noble, whatever things are just, whatever things are pure, whatever things are lovely, whatever things are of good report, if there is any virtue and if there is anything praiseworthy—meditate on these things."*
NKJV. Philippians 4:8.

Heart & Soul

74. *"Change your thoughts and you change your brains..."*
Restak, Richard. (2006). *The Naked Brain: How the Emerging Neurosociety is Changing How We Live, Work, and Love.* p. 131.
New York, NY: Harmony Books.

75. *"As he thinks in his heart, so he is."*
NKJV. Proverbs 23:7.

76. *"Your heart is in constant communication with your brain..."*
Leaf, Caroline. (2009). *Who Switched Off My Brain?* p. 62.
Southlake, Texas: Inprov, LTD.

Chapter 3: Forgiveness & Spirit

Thinking About God

77. *"We are not humans having a spiritual experience. We are spiritual beings having a human experience."*

    Teilhard de Chardin, Pierre.

    Retrieved from: https://www.brainyquote.com/quotes/pierre_teilhard_de_chardi_160888

78. *"Then Jesus said, "Father, forgive them, for they do not know what they do."*

    NKJV. Luke 23:30.

79. *"For the wages of sin is death, but the gift of God is eternal life in Christ Jesus our Lord."*

    NKJV. Romans 6:23.

80. *"He is faithful and just to forgive us our sins and to cleanse us from all unrighteousness."*

    NKJV. 1 John 1:9.

81. Dr. Henry Stapp quoted by Dr. Jeffrey Schwartz.

    Schwartz, Jeffrey & Begley, Sharon. (2002). *The Mind & The Brain.* p. 276

    New York, NY: HarperCollins Publishers.

82. *"If you think about God long enough, something surprising happens..."*

    Newberg, Andrew & Waldman, Mark. (2009). *How God Changes Your Brain: Breakthrough Findings from a Leading Neuroscientist.* p. 3.

    New York, NY: Ballantine Books.

83. *"...heart burn within us..."*

    NKJV. Luke 24:32.

Power of Prayer

84. *"The effectual fervent prayer of a righteous man avails much."*

NKJV. James 5:16

85. *"When we deliberately, intentionally, and purposefully focus on God..."*

Schwartz, Jeffrey & Begley, Sharon. (2002). *The Mind & The Brain.* p. 361.

New York, NY: HarperCollins Publishers.

86. Levy, David & Kilpatrick, Joel. (2011). *Gray Matter: A Neurosurgeon Discovers the Power of Prayer... One Patient at a Time.* [Kindle Version]. Loc. 1476.

87. *"When people get prayed for, they get better faster."*

Church, Dawson. (2014). *The Genie in Your Genes.* p. 67.

Santa Rosa, CA: Energy Psychology Press.

88. *"...there are now 250 scientific studies demonstrating the link between prayer..."*

Dossey, Larry. (1997). *Prayer is Good Medicine.* p. 66.

San Francisco, CA: HarperCollins.

89. *"Dr. David Levy, a practicing neurosurgeon..."*

Leaf, Caroline. (2013). *Switch On Your Brain.* p. 114.

Grand Rapids, MI: Baker Books.

90. *"Thomas Oxman at University of Texas Medical School..."*

Church, Dawson. (2014). *The Genie in Your Genes.* p. 67.

Santa Rosa, CA: Energy Psychology Press.

91. *"St. Luke's Medical Center...."*

Ibid. p. 67.

92. *"According to an Israeli study of 1087 physicians..."*

Ibid. p. 216.

93. *"Cardiologist Randolph Byrd designed a test in 1986 for 393 patients..."*

Dossey, Larry. (1997). *Prayer is Good Medicine.* [Kindle Edition]. Loc. 3035.

San Francisco, CA: HarperCollins.

94. Leibovici, Leonard. (2001, December 22, 2001). Effects of remote, retroactive intercessory prayer on outcomes in patients with bloodstream infection: randomized controlled trial. *British Medical Journal.* Retrieved from: https://doi.org/10.1136/bmj.323.7327.1450

Spiritual Warfare

95. *"For if indeed I have forgiven anything, I have forgiven that one for your sakes in the presence of Christ, let Satan should take advantage of us; for we are not ignorant of his devices."*

NKJV. 2 Corinthians 10:10-11.

96. *"For the weapons of our warfare are not carnal, but mighty in God for pulling down strongholds, casting down arguments and every high thing that exalts itself against the knowledge of God..."*

NKJV. 2 Corinthians 10:4-5.

97. *"Resist the devil and he will flee from you."*

NKJV. James 4:7.

98. *"Therefore, take up the whole armor of God, that you may be able to stand in the evil day, and having done all, to stand."*

NKJV. Ephesians 6:13.

99. *"And Jesus came and spoke to them saying, 'All authority has been given to me in heaven and on earth. Go, therefore and make disciples of all nations...'"*

NKJV. Matthew 28:18-19.

100. *"and they overcame him by the blood of the lamb and the word of their testimony…"*
NKJV. Revelation 12:11.

101. *"For if indeed I have forgiven anything, I have forgiven that one for your sakes in the presence of Christ, let Satan should take advantage of us; for we are not ignorant of his devices."*
NKJV. 2 Corinthians 10:10-11.

Fear

102. *"…our brains are more affected by negative than positive information."*
Restak, Richard. (2006). *The Naked Brain: How the Emerging Neurosociety is Changing How We Live, Work, and Love.* p. 80.
New York, NY: Harmony Books.

103. *"trigger more than 1,400 physical and chemical responses…"*
Leaf, Caroline. (2009). *Who Switched Off My Brain?* pp. 36-37.
Southlake, Texas: Inprov, LTD.

104. *"Let not your heart be troubled, neither let it be afraid."*
NKJV. John 14:27.

105. *"God does not give us the spirit of fear but of power, love and a sound mind."*
NKJV. 2 Timothy 1:7.

106. *"The thief does not come except to steal, and to kill, and to destroy."*
NKJV. John 10:10.

107. *"casting all your care upon Him, because He cares for you."*
NKJV. 1 Peter 5:7.

108. *"We are not slaves to the automatic responses..."*
Restak, Richard. (2006). *The Naked Brain: How the Emerging Neurosociety is Changing How We Live, Work, and Love.* p. 89.
New York, NY: Harmony Books.

Intercession

109. *"...faith is the hand that receives the gift from God."*
Yoemans, Lilian. (2006). *His Healing Power.* p. 14.
Tulsa, Oklahoma: Harrison House.

110. *"For the weapons of our warfare are not carnal, but mighty through God..."*
NKJV. 2 Corinthians 10:4-5.

111. Prince, Joseph. (2018). *Be Christ-Conscious.* Joseph Prince Ministries.
Retrieved from: https://www.josephprince.org/blog/daily-grace-inspirations/be-christ-conscious

112. *"I have forgiven that one for your sakes in the presence of Christ, lest Satan should take advantage of us; for we are not ignorant of his devices."*
NKJV. 2 Corinthians 2:11.

113. *"Resist the devil and he will flee from you."*
NKJV. James 4:7.

114. *"...we keep Satan from getting an advantage over us."*
NKJV. 2 Corinthians 2:11.

Deliverance

115. *"releasing a person's will..."*
Hammond, Frank & Ida Mae. (1973). *Pigs in the Parlor: A Practical Guide to Deliverance.* p. 63.
Kirkwood, MO: Impact Books.

116. *"The nature of evil is the impulse to power over others."*
Burke, L. Morrill. University of Southern Maine, English Department. *College Writing,* Fall, 1975.

117. *"...to destroy the works of the devil...."*
NKJV. 1 John 3:8.

118. *"...liberty to the captives."*
NKJV. Luke 4:18.

119. *"Mr A had been tormented for twelve years..."*
Hammond, Frank & Ida Mae. (1973). *Pigs in the Parlor: A Practical Guide to Deliverance.* p. 54.
Kirkwood, MO: Impact Books.

120. *"Deliverance Prayer."*
Hammond, Frank & Ida Mae. (1973). *Pigs in the Parlor: A Practical Guide to Deliverance.* p. 107.
Kirkwood, MO: Impact Books.

Chapter 4: Forgiving Others

121. *"Forgive us our debts even as we forgive our debtors."*
NKJV. Matthew 6:12.

122. *"Let all bitterness, wrath, anger, clamor, and evil speaking..."*
NKJV. Ephesians 4:31.

Forgive & Forget

123. *"We love Him because He first loved us."*
NKJV. 1 John 4:19.

124. *"As far as the east is from the west, so far has he removed our transgressions from us."*
NKJV. Psalm 103:12.

125. *"Their sins and lawless deeds I will remember no more."*
NKJV. Hebrews 10:17.

Justice

126. *"...an eye for an eye..."*

    NKJV. Matthew 5:38.

127. Leaf, Caroline & Levy, David, Dr. (2018). *"Faith, forgiveness, and the mind with Dr. David Levy."* [You Tube]. Retrieved from: https://www.youtube.com/watch?v=FjbotdXZLvQ

128. Luskin, Fred. (2010). *Forgive For Good: A Proven Prescription for Health and Happiness.* Quoting Frederick Buechner. p. 77.

    New York, NY: HarperCollins.

Chapter 5: Forgiving Ourselves

129. *"There is therefore now no condemnation to those who are in Christ Jesus..."*

    NKJV. Romans 8:1.

130. *"...hidden in Christ."*

    NKJV. Colossians 3:3.

131. *"...for the joy that was set before Him..."*

    NKJV. Hebrews 12:2.

132. *"As Joseph Prince teaches... all of our sins were in the future."*

    Prince, Joseph. (2000). *Forgiven Of Past, Present And Future Sins.*

    Retrieved from: https://www.josephprince.com/sermon/forgiven-of-past-present-and-future-sins?sku=20000730M3

133. *"He died once for all."*

    NKJV. Hebrews 10:10.

134. *"...no condemnation..."*

    NKJV. Romans 8:1.

135. *"...faithful and just to forgive us of our sins..."*
     NKJV. 1 John 1:9.

136. *"Jesus came to destroy the works of the devil."*
     NKJV. 1 John 3:8.

137. *"All authority has been given to Me in heaven and on earth."*
     NKJV. Matthew 28:18.

138. Johnson, Bill. (2017.) *How God Sees Me.* [YouTube].
     Retrieved from: https://www.youtube.com/watch?v=SEKGhdbbe1Y

Chapter 6: Forgiving God

Relationship with God

139. Copeland, Kenneth. (May 30, 2015). *What Happens to My Brain When I Don't Forgive?* [Youtube].
     Retrieved from: https://www.youtube.com/watch?v=elYqeDNm14g

140. *"promote relational repair with God"*
     Toussaint, Loren; Worthington, Everett, Jr. & Williams, David. (2015). *Forgiveness and Health.* p. 44.
     New York, NY: Springer.

141. *"If you believe God loves you, it's an enormously protective factor."*
     Church, Dawson, PhD. (2014). *The Genie in Your Genes.* p. 65.
     Santa Rosa, CA: Energy Psychology Press.

142. *"...view of God cure for 10,000..."*
     Tozer, A. W. (1961). *Knowledge of the Holy.* p. 4.
     San Francisco: CA: HarperCollins.

143. *"...for the joy set before him..."*
     NKJV. Hebrews 12:2.

144. *"Greater love has no one than this, than to lay down one's life for his friends."*

NKJV. John 15:13.

145. *"Unforgiveness strains and tears at all our relationships... including God."*

Toussaint, Loren; Worthington, Everett, Jr. & Williams, David. (2015). *Forgiveness and Health.* p. 79.

New York, NY: Springer.

146. *"Research studies show that unforgiveness toward God causes high levels of stress and depression."*

Ibid. p. 79.

147. *"And I will restore to you the years that the locust hath eaten, the cankerworm, and the caterpillar, and the palmerworm, my great army which I sent among you."*

NKJV. Joel 2:25.

The Good Father

148. Ellis, Jeffrey. (2014). *Forgiving God.*

Maitland, FL: Xulon Press.

Chapter 7: Unforgiveness

149. Levy, David & Kilpatrick, Joel. (2011). *Gray Matter: A Neurosurgeon Discovers the Power of Prayer... One Patient at a Time.* [Kindle Version]. Loc. 1476.

150. *"The root of bitterness..."*

NKJV. Hebrews 12:15.

Unforgiveness: Health Effects

151. *"Unforgiveness has serious negative health effects, especially in older adults."*

Seawell, Asani; Toussaint, Loren & Cheadle, Alyssa. "Prospective associations between unforgiveness and physical health and positive mediating mechanisms in a nationally representative sample of older adults." *Psychology & Health,* (2013). p. 3.

152. *"These include higher heart rate, blood pressure, stress..."*
Ibid. p. 3.

153. *arterial sclerosis, hypertension, angina..."*
Toussaint, Loren & Cheadle, Alyssa. "Unforgivness and the Broken Heart: Unforgiving Tendencies, Problems Due to Unforgiveness, and 12-month Prevalence of Cardiovascular Health Conditions." *Religion and Psychology.* (2009).
Nova Science Publishers, p. 23.

154. *"The consequences of allowing the root of bitterness..."*
Hammond, Frank. (1995). *Forgiving Others: The Key to Healing and Deliverance.*
Kirkwood, MO: Impact Christian Books.

155. *"Everett Worthington describes these health effects:"*
Worthington, Everett, Jr. (2005). *The Power of Forgiving.* [Kindle Edition]. Loc. 242.
Philadelphia, PA: Templeton Foundation Press.

156. Leaf, Caroline & Levy, David. (2018). *"Forgiveness & the mind-body connection."* [YouTube]. Retrieved from: https://www.youtube.com/watch?v=kBom9ewEIiU

Quid Pro Quo

157. *"Forgive us our debts as we forgive our debtors."*
NKJV. Matthew 6:12.

158. *"If we confess our sins to Jesus, He is faithful and just to forgive us our sins..."*
NKJV. 1 John 1:9.

159. *"We think we're hurting the other person, but actually it's hurting us..."*
Leaf, Caroline & Levy, David. (2018). *"Forgiveness & the mind-body connection."* [You Tube].
Retrieved from: https://www.youtube.com/watch?v=kBom9ewEIiU

160. *"Those who are forgiven much..."*

NKJV. Luke 7:47.

161. *"And be kind to one another, tenderhearted, forgiving one another...."*

NKJV. Ephesians 4:32.

The Unforgiving Servant

162. *"The most common thing that will prevent a person from receiving deliverance is unforgiveness."*

Hammond, Frank & Ida Mae. (1973). *Pigs in the Parlor: A Practical Guide to Deliverance.* p. 105.

Kirkwood, MO: Impact Books

163. *"Those who have unforgiveness toward anyone else, dead or alive, cannot be delivered."*

Ibid. p. 119.

164. *"Unforgiveness puts us in the custody of tormenting spirits."*

Hammond, Frank. (1995). *Forgiving Others: The Key to Healing and Deliverance.* p. 24.

Kirkwood, MO: Impact Christian Books.

Entanglement

165. *"In centuries past, the punishment for murder was to chain the murderer..."*

Hammond, Frank. (1995). *Forgiving Others: The Key to Healing and Deliverance.* p. 18.

Kirkwood, MO: Impact Christian Books.

166. *"If someone has hurt you and are 1000 miles away..."*

Leaf, Caroline. (August 20, 2017). *"Forgiveness and Mind Is Related."* [YouTube]

Retrieved from: https://www.youtube.com/watch?v=eTEAtaDOeTU

167. *"When we forgive them, we can remove them from our head."*

Leaf, Caroline. (June 5, 2015). *"What Happens to My Brain When I Forgive?"*

Retrieved from: https://www.youtube.com/watch?v=elYqeDNm14g

168. *"Beloved, never avenge yourselves.... Vengeance is Mine..."*

Amplified Bible. (1984). Romans 12:19.

169. Burke, L. Morrill, PhD. University of Southern Maine, English Department.

College Writing, Fall, 1975.

170. *"In 2004, Leanna Standish of Bastyr University conducted an experiment..."*

Radin, Dean. (2006). *Entangled Minds.* p. 139.

New York, NY: Pocket Books.

171. *"Dean Radin designed a fascinating experiment."*

Church, Dawson. (2014). *The Genie in Your Genes.* p. 202.

Santa Rosa, CA: Energy Psychology Press.

172. *"Einstein's spooky actions at a distance..."*

Rosenblum, Bruce & Kuttner, Fred. (2006). *Quantum Enigma.* p. 151.

New York, NY: Oxford University Press.

173. *"Events at the edge of the galaxy influence what happens at the edge of your garden."*

Rosenblum, Bruce & Kuttner, Fred. (2006). *Quantum Enigma.* p. 139.

New York, NY: Oxford University Press.

Concluding Thoughts

Salvation

174. *"God so loved the world..."*
NKJV. John 3:16.

175. *"But He was wounded* for *our* transgressions, *He was* bruised for *our iniquities."*
NKJV. Isaiah 53:5.

176. *"He told me I was His son."*
NKJV. Psalm 2:7.

177. *"For you died, and your life is* hidden *with* Christ *in God."*
NKJV. Colossians 3:3.

178. *"sons and daughters of God..."*
NKJV. John 1:11.

179. *"The Lord will perfect that which concerns me;"*
NKJV. Psalm 138:8.

About the Author

Jeffrey Ellis is the best-selling author of *Forgiving God* and *Pure Leadership*. He has a Master's degree from Abilene Christian University in Abilene, Texas. Ellis served on the Board of Directors of Wayside Cross Ministries, Global Action, and Journey Family Church. He has served as a volunteer prison chaplain since 2003 and received the State of Illinois Volunteer of the Year award from the Illinois Department of Corrections in 2005.

A father of six and grandfather of fourteen, he and his wife, Ginger, reside in Southwest Michigan. He and Ginger are volunteer chaplains at Van Buren and Allegan County jails. He is a sought-after speaker on faith, leadership, and forgiveness.

Jeffrey Ellis can be reached at:
https://www.facebook.com/ForgivingGod

96027113R00066

Made in the USA
Lexington, KY
15 August 2018